PERFORMANCE WITHOUT PRESSURE

PERFORMANCE WITHOUT PRESSURE

A GUIDE FOR PARENTS

Martin L. Seldman, Ph.D.

Walker and Company New York

First published in the United States of America in 1988 by the Walker Publishing Company, Inc.

Published simultaneously in Canada by Thomas Allen & Son Canada, Limited, Markham, Ontario.

Book design by Laurie McBarnette

Library of Congress Cataloging-in-Publication Data

Seldman, Martin L.
    Performance without pressure.

    Bibliography: p.
    Includes index.
    1. Parenting—United States—Psychological aspects.
2. Parents—United States—Attitudes. 3. Performance.
4. Self-respect. I. Title.
HQ755.83.S44   1988   649'.1   87-35826
ISBN 0-8027-1022-0
ISBN 0-8027-7311-7 (pbk.)

Printed in the United States of America

10 9 8 7 6 5 4 3 2 1

To my parents, Zelda and Fred;
my children, Allison and Joshua;
and to Neil Seldman of the Institute of Local Self-Reliance and
the members of the Institute of Cultural Affairs who tirelessly
work to promote equality and opportunity for all individuals

ACKNOWLEDGMENTS

This book draws upon the ideas and research of many individuals. In particular, I'm indebted to the self-talk research of Dr. Maxie Maultsby, Jr., and Dr. Donald Meichenbaum, the "possibility thinking" concepts of Reverend Robert Schuller, and Stewart Emery's work on "the attitude of a learner."

My companion in the development of many of the Performance Without Pressure (PWP) principles and skills is Sandy Smith. I am especially grateful for the love and humor he brings to his work.

Susan and Chuck Neder have presented many of the PWP concepts to thousands of parents and youth workers throughout the United States. Their feedback, support, and encouragement have been invaluable.

Finally, I want to express deep appreciation to my editors, Karen Feinberg and Kristine Karnezis, and to Dr. Bob Bolton for his unwavering honesty.

CONTENTS

INTRODUCTION 1

1 SELF-ESTEEM: ACHIEVEMENT PLUS
   ACCEPTANCE 6

2 THE CYCLES OF UNDERACHIEVEMENT
   AND ACHIEVEMENT 15

3 THE POWER OF SELF-TALK 30

4 LEARNING TO LEARN 40

5 IDENTIFYING STRENGTHS AND
   POTENTIAL 58

6 ACQUIRING SKILLS BY SETTING GOALS 80

7 POSITIVE SELF-MOTIVATION 101

8 BUILDING RESPONSIBILITY AND SELF-
   DISCIPLINE 116

9 PROBLEM-SOLVING AND TEST-TAKING
   SKILLS 134

10 POSITIVE PREPARATION THROUGH
   MENTAL REHEARSAL 143

11 SELF-MANAGEMENT SKILLS: NOT MAKING
A PROBLEM OUT OF A PROBLEM *155*

12 THE SELF-TALK OF IMPROVEMENT:
LEARNING FROM EXPERIENCE *165*

REFERENCES AND
RECOMMENDED READINGS *177*

INDEX *181*

PERFORMANCE
WITHOUT
PRESSURE

INTRODUCTION

Twenty years ago, before I became a parent—even before I became a clinical psychologist—something happened that sparked my desire to write about children, performance, and pressure. Early in my graduate training I was doing intelligence testing on a bright first-grade boy who was desperate to do well. When time for a task ran out, he pleaded to work on it more. If he didn't arrange a block design correctly, he swore he could get it right and begged to try it again. Finally, in his anxiety to avoid making mistakes, he tried to cheat. I tried to reassure him with the truth. He was doing well. I told him that nobody gets all the block designs in the time allowed, but nothing I said seemed to reduce his internal pressure. The little boy's darting eyes and troubled face affected me deeply. Why was he so desperate for perfect performance? What were his parents' expectations? Would this pressure to achieve help him or hurt him in developing his talents and potential?

THE PRESSURE TO ACHIEVE
Most of us have a strong desire to instill in our children the motivation to develop their abilities. We want them to have the skills and strategies that will prepare them for their futures. In many families the concern for children's achievements has intensified, fueled by the desire to prepare

a child for increased competition in school, sports, or employment. Recently a *U.S. News and World Report* survey on colleges drew so much attention that 458,000 reprints were ordered. Deputy Editor Larry Maloney commented on the overwhelming response, "In a highly competitive environment, people are always looking for an edge, for themselves or their children."

As parents and children respond to these achievement pressures, more and more youngsters are experiencing stress symptoms. Dr. David Elkind, author of *The Hurried Child*, an instant best-seller about children who undergo too much pressure to succeed, warns: "Hurried children are stressed by the fear of failure—of not achieving fast enough or high enough." He relates these rising pressures to a variety of childhood problems, as indicated by the dramatic increase in teenage suicide. For example, for millions of girls in the United States, the pressure to be thin is now starting in grade school. Inappropriate dieting and eating disorders such as anorexia and bulimia are now epidemic among females from the sixth grade through college.

THE PARENTAL DILEMMA: PERFORMANCE WITHOUT PRESSURE

Many concerned parents struggle daily with this dilemma: They want their children to be competent and capable and confident in themselves, yet they are not sure how to instill those qualities without creating the excessive pressures that will block those very goals.

This book offers specific methods and skills to help parents work to resolve this dilemma. The focus is on equipping children with the skills and attitudes they need to develop their full potential. The constant goal will be to put your child on the path to *achievement* and *acceptance*, two cornerstones to a healthy self-esteem.

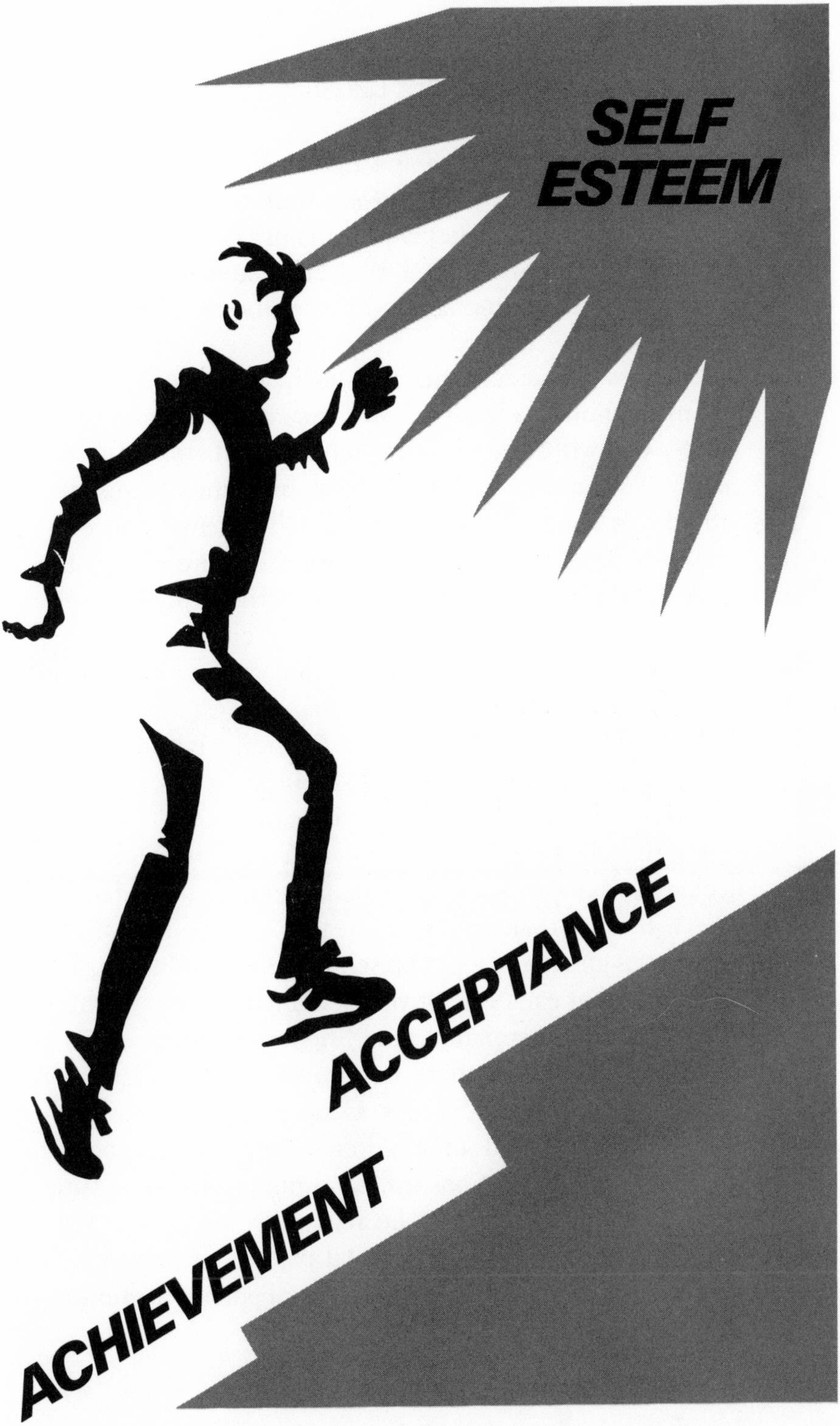
SELF
ESTEEM
ACCEPTANCE
ACHIEVEMENT

In this book I share what I have learned from working with children, parents, educators, counselors, clergy, athletes, entrepreneurs, salespeople, and professional speakers. For the past twenty years I've been a student of human performance and potential, and I've included research from varied fields.

I discuss skills and attitudes—such as love of learning, self-motivation, problem solving, responsibility, and discipline—that will serve you and your family members for the rest of your lives. A key to developing these skills and attitudes is learning about *self-talk*, the mental conversations we have with ourselves, discussed throughout the book. The parenting techniques I describe will help your children achieve in school, sports, or creative activities, while teaching them to become self-accepting by dealing with mistakes, failures, and performance pressures.

Each of the methods and skills I describe is within your reach. And with motivation and practice you can adopt the attitudes and mental habits you will learn about.

You should evaluate the information and skills I offer and decide what makes sense for you and your family. Many of you will find that you are already using some of the techniques and approaches presented here. In addition, I'm convinced that each one of you could teach me something about being a better parent, and I hope you will do so.

Keep in mind that there is no one set of standards for being a good parent. Stanley Coopersmith, an early researcher in the field of children's self-esteem, reported many hard facts about positive parenting in his book *Antecedents of Self-Esteem*. Yet he remarks, "We should note that there are virtually no parental patterns of behavior or parental attitudes that are common to all parents of children with high self-esteem."

IMPROVEMENT, NOT PERFECTION

Likewise, remember that improvement, not perfection, should be your goal. Perfection is elusive in most endeavors; in parenting it is impossible. Our children's behavior is influenced by many factors that we can't control: individual temperament, genetics, society, peer pressure, media, and much more. Thus I invite you to learn the methods I describe and teach them to your children with the goal of improvement and progress.

TEACHING YOURSELF FIRST

The best way to instill attitudes and develop habits in your child is to acquire them yourself. In *Raising Positive Kids in a Negative World*, Zig Ziglar states, "The only way to raise positive kids is to start by becoming a positive parent."

This book is designed as a guide for attitude development and skill training. I suggest that you read it through with your child in mind, but also think about your own achievements, pressures, and potential. When you apply to yourself the principles I discuss, most of the task of teaching your child will already be accomplished.

Most parents want a great deal for their children and sacrifice in many ways. Yet we know that good intentions don't automatically produce good results. Ironically, some of our best intentions and expectations can work against our goals for our children. Each of us has a range of expectations for ourselves and our families. If these are too low we never really grasp a vision of what is possible for us. If we have high expectations but don't back them up with the necessary skills and attitudes, we are vulnerable to feelings of frustration and inadequacy. Therefore, my overriding goal is to enable you to develop a vision of your child's potential and to construct a clear path to reaching that potential.

CHAPTER 1

SELF-ESTEEM: ACHIEVEMENT PLUS ACCEPTANCE

NO SIGNIFICANT ASPECT OF OUR THINKING, MOTIVATION,
FEELINGS OR BEHAVIOR IS UNAFFECTED BY
SELF-EVALUATION.

NATHANIEL BRANDEN
Honoring The Self

Our view of ourselves is a collection of beliefs about our traits, characteristics, and abilities. Self-esteem is the evaluative aspect of those beliefs.

Am I good, bad, acceptable, or adequate?
Am I good enough or do I need to be better?
Can I learn?
Can I cope with problems?
Am I as good as other people?
What do mistakes and failures say about me?
Do I respect myself?
Can I make a significant contribution?
Do I count?

These are all self-esteem questions. As children grow, they shape their answers to these questions.

Healthy, productive self-esteem has two essential cornerstones: *achievement* and *acceptance*. Each needs to be pursued as a goal in itself to increase the chances that our children will be effective and happy. The attitudes and skills I discuss in this book will help you reach those goals.

THE COMPETENCY MOTIVE AND ACHIEVEMENT

Dr. Robert White, a pioneer in motivation research, labeled our inner desire to master skills and tasks as *competency motivation*. His research revealed that human beings have a need for mastery and competence, including the desire to cope with their environment and affect it positively. People want to be effective whether they are three or eighty-three, and White used the term *effectance* to describe this motivation. Effectance and its corollary, achievement, form one cornerstone of self-esteem. Children with high levels of self-esteem feel competent. They believe they can learn and improve. At some level, in some arena, they have achieved success; they are encouraged.

A major part of this book is focused on achievement. Drawing upon the latest research in education, coaching, child development, sports psychology, and the study of peak performance, I present skills and methods that you can use every day to help your child explore and develop his or her abilities.

THE NEED FOR ACCEPTANCE

Competence and achievement are important but they don't guarantee self-esteem. To realize a deep and enduring self-esteem, children need another cornerstone, *acceptance*. They need to believe that they possess a worth and a value separate from their skills and abilities. This belief is not easy to instill in anyone, especially children, because children are vulnerable to discouragement, which can take many forms:

They play with older siblings, cousins or friends who may
be better at school or sports.

Mentally and physically they develop in spurts and may
struggle for a while until they master new tasks and skills.

Their daily life contains many mistakes and misses.

When other kids or adults tease them, make fun of their
shortcomings, or call them names, a part of them starts
to believe negative things about themselves.

In reality, none of us is good at everything. Even in the
areas where we do well, eventually someone will come
along who is better. Sometimes we will make a poor grade,
miss a shot, or hit the wrong key. At times we won't reach
our goals and we will be disappointed with our performance. Sometimes we will reach a plateau, where we work
hard at something but don't seem to get any better; we may
even feel that we are getting worse.

We need to alter the equation "my achievements = my
self-worth," or self-esteem will be on the line with every
performance. If our self-worth depends solely on our accomplishments and proficiencies, we are on shaky ground.
We wonder: "Do I have to be perfect?" "Am I always being
measured?" Self-acceptance is the safety valve that helps a
human being deal with the pressure to perform.

Unless we can build acceptance into the self-esteem
equation, we run the risk of blocking even our children's
achievement goals. In her classic book, *Your Child's Self-
Esteem*, Dorothy C. Briggs reports, "The commonest cause
of learning blocks, particularly in children from middle-
class families, comes from undue pressure to achieve goals
beyond their reach." In the chapters ahead I share skills
and techniques that you can use to help your child acquire
self-acceptance. The first key is to help them experience
love without having to achieve to win it.

Worlds Without Achievement

Parents who express genuine pleasure upon seeing their child progress and learn are reinforcing the child's desire to succeed. Research into the characteristics of children who achieve success demonstrates the importance of displaying approval for accomplishments.

However, there is a need for *balance*. Children who are listened to, and who receive *attention* and *affection* at moments that don't involve striving, will also learn that their parents' love doesn't rise and fall with their latest performance. It's enduring. The goal is to help the child accept the idea that there are worlds without achievement. This realization removes a great deal of the pressure to perform and allows the child's inner desire to explore, master, and enjoy activities to merge with his or her need for parental approval.

Accepting Mistakes and Imperfections

From cradle to grave, our lives contain mistakes, setbacks, and imperfections. They are not limited to the young. I remember lecturing my daughter about losing things, and then two days later informing her sheepishly that I had lost my wallet in a movie theater.

An essential ingredient of your child's ability to perform without pressure will be the positive, realistic, productive attitudes he or she adopts about mistakes and poor performances. In Chapter 4 I explore in depth the attitude of a learner. This attitude allows children to try new activities because they aren't afraid to fail. They accept mistakes and setbacks as part of the acquisition of skills and know how to turn mistakes into lessons. They use their time and energy for discovering solutions, solving problems, and finding the keys to improvement, not for self-punishment.

To learn the ability to forgive and accept themselves, our children need to experience forgiveness and acceptance from the important adults in their lives. Margo Maine, assistant clinical director at Newington Children's Hospital in Connecticut, has researched the low self-esteem patterns of adolescent girls who suffer from anorexia nervosa. She advises parents, and fathers in particular, "Help your daughter to see herself as OK no matter what she weighs. Then she'll be less susceptible to cultural influences that lead her to drive for thinness and view emaciation as beautiful."

THE SKILLS AND ATTITUDES IN ACTION

The following text is an example of some of the skills and attitudes of achievement and acceptance as used by two seventh-graders, Andrea and Jim, cousins in junior high school.

Andrea has a 78 average in algebra and works hard at learning the material. Jim, who spends a lot of his time playing basketball, has found that if he pays attention in class, he can do his algebra homework on the bus. Solving math problems is fun for him and he usually scores in the 90s on tests without special studying.

The midyear exams are scheduled. Let's look at Andrea's thoughts and actions.

Jim aces these math tests without even studying. It comes so easy to him. It's kind of discouraging to study so hard and still not do as well as he does, but that's just the way it is. I've got to work hard to learn the rules and equations but eventually I get it. There are things that are easy for me, like writing stories, that Jim has a hard time with. I've got to figure out what I need to do to be prepared for this test and not worry about Jim's grades or how he studies.

Andrea reviewed all the types of problems that were going to be on the test. After realizing that she didn't know how to do a certain type of problem, she overcame her embarrassment and stayed after class to ask her teacher about it.

The afternoon before the test, Andrea worked on the problems that were hard for her and then asked Jim to come over and check her work. He did, and even pointed out some ways of solving the problems that the teacher hadn't explained.

That night as she lay in bed, Andrea mentally rehearsed, step by step, how she was going to take the test the next day. She pictured herself relaxed but alert, working carefully through the problems and solving them correctly. She also prepared herself mentally to deal with difficulties by imagining herself getting stuck on a problem but staying calm and confident about solving the others.

In math class the next day, Andrea took advantage of the few moments before the teacher gave out the test. She said to herself:

I'm prepared and ready for this test. It's kind of fun to use what I know to solve problems. I've got a plan for how I'm going to take the test and I'll stick to it. I'm not going to worry about any that I miss. I've paid attention in class, studied hard, received help, and now all I can do is give it my best. If I get some problems wrong, I'll learn what I need to know after the test.

Andrea felt some butterflies in her stomach and she was anxious to get started. The test contained twenty problems, including some written out in words that gave her trouble. Sticking to her test-taking strategy, Andrea skipped over the tough problems and worked first on the ones that she was confident she could solve. After completing those, she attacked the hard problems with some success. She worked one problem through, but when she checked her answers in the original equation she realized they were wrong. She said to herself:

> *Where did I go wrong? OK, calm down. It's just an error. Let's get back on track. Just do what Jim said to do if this happens.*

Andrea solved nineteen problems to her satisfaction. After the test she said to herself:

> *I did it! The hard work paid off. I stuck to my plan and even sailed through that mistake on number 11. I just need to ask Jim about the problem I didn't get.*

The next week Andrea got back her test score, an 89. She was very proud of herself, and started to believe she could get an A in algebra.

Jim also did well on the test. Math tests were fun for him, but at that time the focus of his life was the seventh-grade basketball team, on which he was a starting guard.

One Sunday afternoon there was a game against their closest rivals, currently the best team in the league. A good-sized crowd was on hand, made up of parents, teachers, and children from both schools. The game was exciting. The boys played hard and the lead changed hands many times.

Jim gave the game all he had. He hustled up and down the court and made several baskets that kept the game close. In the final seconds of the game, Jim's team, trailing by one point, got the ball and brought it down court. The other guard passed the ball to Jim, and with two seconds left, Jim took a ten-foot jump shot and missed. The game was over; Jim's team had lost. As he walked off the court, Jim heard some of his classmates booing him in the stands. They yelled, "You blew it. You lost the game."

Jim was hurt and disappointed, but he said to himself:

> *Those jokers in the stands ought to cool it. They're up there taking cheap shots. I'm down here on the team, going for it. They're watchers. I'm a player.*
>
> *I wanted to make that shot. I could have made it. It hurts to lose. We played hard and we could have been in first place. But I didn't lose the game. The team lost; it just came down to my shot.*
>
> *I think I did rush the shot, and I didn't have to. I didn't set up like I usually do. I'll just have to learn how to take my regular shot even with two seconds left.*
>
> *All in all, I played a pretty good game. I know I tried as hard as I could. I'll get a lot more chances to make important shots.*

Andrea and Jim demonstrated some of the attitudes and methods that you will learn about in the following chapters. These include:

Problem solving
Preparation and planning
Mental rehearsal
Self-motivation
Openness to feedback
Attitude of a learner
Stress inoculation
Self-management
Self-instructions
Calm self-critique
Focus on possibilities

There are many other attitudes as well that promote confidence, love of learning, acquisition of skills, persistence, problem solving, responsibility, discipline, motivation, and self-acceptance. It's never too late to change habits and acquire new skills. Throughout this book I explain the methods for acquiring these attitudes yourself and show you how to teach them to your children.

Obviously, Andrea and Jim didn't just wake up one day and know how to prepare mentally, self-start, and cope with difficult situations as they did in this example. Attitudes are mental habits; repetition and practice are essential for learning. Andrea, Jim, and their parents worked at these habits. Fortunately, they can be taught in many ways, in a wide variety of situations. They are simple enough to make sense even to a five-year-old.

THE CYCLES OF UNDERACHIEVEMENT AND ACHIEVEMENT

ONE PERSON SAYS "I CAN DO IT," ANOTHER PERSON SAYS "I CAN'T DO IT," AND THEY ARE BOTH RIGHT.

HENRY FORD

OUR DOUBTS ARE TRAITORS; MAKING US LOSE THE GOOD WE OFT MIGHT WIN; BY FEARING TO ATTEMPT.

SHAKESPEARE
Measure for Measure

In 1973 Carol Dweck and N. Dickon Reppucci, research psychologists, conducted an experiment on persistence and achievement in fifth-grade children. All the students were motivated and capable, and each was asked to complete a series of block designs. Two adults alternated in assigning the designs. One adult gave problems that the children could solve (the "success" experimenter), and the other gave unsolvable problems (the "failure" experimenter).

At a certain point in the experiment, the "failure" experimenter started to assign *solvable* designs. The dramatic finding was that almost half the students didn't complete the designs she assigned, *even though they were now working on problems they* were *capable of solving.* At the same time, they continued to solve similar problems given by the "success" presenter. In other words, they gave up on problems assigned by the "failure" adult. The researchers say,

"In essence [these children] are saying to themselves that whether they try or not the consequences will be the same."

Further work with the children who persisted and succeeded as well as those who gave up and failed revealed significant differences in their attitudes. The persistent group believed that results depend on one's own actions, particularly effort. They were likely to attribute failure to lack of effort.

The other group tended to attribute success or failure to ability. They reasoned, "Either you can do it or you can't." In this situation they believed that they couldn't solve any of the problems offered by the "failure" adult, so they quit. They lost their motivation when faced with problems from this adult.

In reality, however, they were capable of success. Until the change, both groups had performed equally well; some of the children who didn't persist actually had been doing better than the others.

Dweck went on to develop a training procedure to help children learn to persist. When children didn't solve a problem they could have solved, they were told, "You should have tried harder." She was successful at teaching them that failure can be overcome.

These studies demonstrate the vital impact of children's attitudes and beliefs on their performance. Our beliefs affect our emotions and motivation. Motivation affects effort and actions. Effort contributes to results. Then, as we all know, our results reinforce or alter our beliefs. This cycle of cause and effect is illustrated in Figure 1, the performance cycle.

These cycles are repeated over and over in school, at home, and on the playground. Negative cycles lead to poor performance and withdrawal; positive cycles generate confidence, optimism, and success.

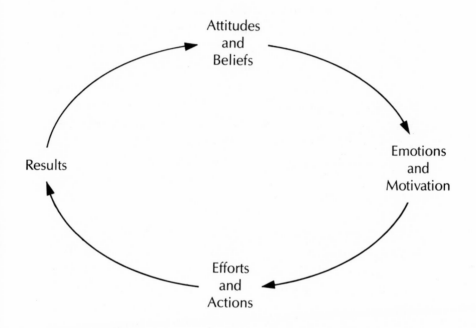

FIGURE 1. **The Performance Cycle**

THE UNDERACHIEVEMENT CYCLE

The underachievement cycle in Figure 2 is an example of a negative cycle. It shows how a belief can become a self-fulfilling prophecy and illustrates the wisdom of Henry Ford's statement quoted at the beginning of this chapter. Our beliefs about our abilities often become realities.

I went to a public school in Brooklyn, where the sixth-grade classes held a group sing every year. One day, when 150 of us were rehearsing in the auditorium, the teacher stopped the singing and pointed to me in the back row. "Young man," she announced, "when we sing please just move your lips. Don't let any noise come out."

I was traumatized by my first dose of feedback about my singing. How often do you think I sang in public after that? How much better do you think I got? I'm sure you can guess the answers.

Some of you are probably thinking, "Well, maybe he just can't sing." The point is that I'll never know if I don't do it and receive feedback or instruction. In fact, I stayed away from music and singing until recently, when my children began to learn about it.

How much can a person improve at activities that he doesn't put effort into? This is what Shakespeare meant by "failing to attempt." The underachievement cycle becomes a self-perpetuating reality: I don't believe I can do something or do it well enough. I make little or no effort. I resist feedback or coaching, and my belief becomes reinforced. "See, I knew I couldn't do it. I'm just no good at it. I'll never be able to do it."

Children are highly susceptible to these beliefs and cycles. Borrowing from the tens column, hitting a baseball, or remembering scales can be difficult tasks for children, whose mental and physical abilities develop unevenly. Dr. Melvin Levine of the University of North Carolina Medical

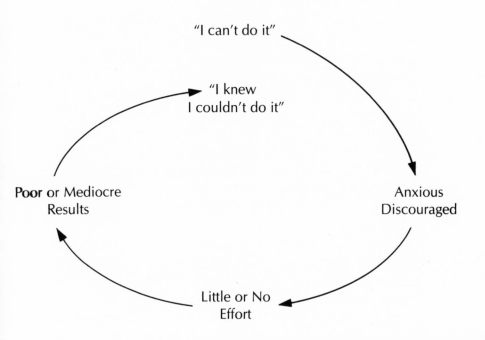

FIGURE 2. **The Underachievement Cycle**

School surveyed 700 children at random and found that seventeen percent had undiagnosed developmental lags in their ability to learn. How often do these situations become "I can't read. I can't learn. I'm just a dummy"?

In later chapters we explore other origins of these negative cycles. Children can become discouraged when they compare themselves to others who have more ability. Nervousness and tension can totally disrupt their efforts. In addition, children are suggestible; they can easily be led to believe that bad names and negative labels are true.

My life hasn't suffered very much without singing, and somehow the world has struggled on without my voice. The decision "I can't sing" did not have serious consequences, but every day children make similar, far more serious decisions that follow the same cycle.

Children can make decisions about their intelligence, attractiveness, creativity, and athletic ability at an early age based on very limited and biased information. These decisions often start negative cycles and set limits that aren't questioned or tested in adult life.

As with any vicious cycle that feeds on itself, we want to stop the underachievement cycle as early as possible. The best choice is to prevent it from happening at all, and we can do that by generating *achievement cycles.*

THE ACHIEVEMENT CYCLE
Figure 3 shows the achievement cycle that, like the underachievement cycle, is self-sustaining. The beliefs in this cycle, however, generate feelings and motivation that produce effort and improvement. "I can do it" becomes "I did it." In the achievement cycle a child not only acquires confidence for a single task but also learns things about effort, setbacks, and persistence that apply to all situations.

Dr. Albert Bandura, of Stanford University, has con-

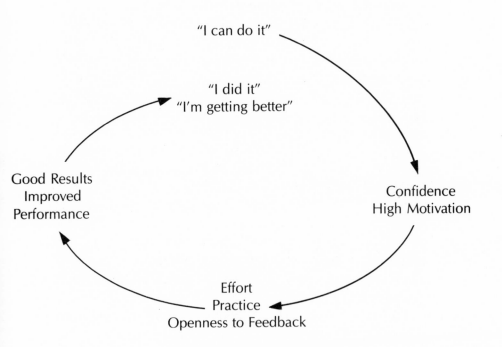

"I can do it"

"I did it"
"I'm getting better"

Good Results
Improved
Performance

Confidence
High Motivation

Effort
Practice
Openness to Feedback

FIGURE 3. **The Achievement Cycle**

ducted research on a concept he calls *self-efficacy*. A child with a high level of self-efficacy has a confidence that goes beyond his or her ability to perform the task at hand. He believes that he can overcome the obstacles, problems, and challenges along the path to higher levels of accomplishment.

My objective is to present methods you can use to develop a sense of self-efficacy in your child, which will produce positive cycles and short-circuit the negative ones. First, however, you must understand in detail the impact of your child's thoughts on his or her actions.

CASE STUDIES AND SELF-TALK

The rest of this chapter contains six case studies involving children in important situations. In each case study, the situation is described and then two versions of how the child talked about it to himself or herself are presented. These two inner monologues are labeled *Self-Talk #1* and *Self-Talk #2*.

Your objective is to think about each child's self-talk and predict the following:

> How would this child probably feel if he talked to himself that way?
> What would her actions probably be?
> What would be the probable results, now and in the future?

Each of these case studies is designed to give you insights into positive and negative self-talk and achievement cycles. In addition, they will give you a preview of some of the performance attitudes and skills you will learn about in later chapters. As you read, think about the possible feelings, actions, and results in each situation.

Case Study 1: The Fourth-Grade Math Test

About halfway through a math test, nine-year-old Jennifer is having difficulty with long-division problems. She has erased her work twice on one problem and is starting to get frustrated and upset.

Self-Talk #1: "I can't get it to check out. Nobody else is having problems. Why can't I get the right answer? My paper looks so messy. Everybody is going to see all my erasing. I hate these tests!"

Self-Talk #2: "It still won't check out! Slow down, Jenny, you're rushing. Don't use all your time on this one problem. Just calm down now. Do it step by step, just like homework. I'll try it once more, and check each step before I go on. If I don't get it right this time, I'll just go on to finish the rest of the test. Miss Robertson can tell me what I'm missing if I ask her after the test."

SELF-TALK #1 REVIEW

If Jennifer had used self-talk #1, what can we guess about her probable feelings, actions, and results?

Feelings: Saying these things to herself, Jennifer is probably feeling a mixture of nervousness, embarrassment, and frustration.

Actions: When Jennifer is talking this way to herself and feeling the way she feels, she is not taking any positive action to solve the troublesome problem or any of the other problems on the test.

Results: Obviously we can't be certain about the results of the test after only a quick glimpse of Jennifer's thoughts and feelings. Still, even though her emotions are understandable, it is easy to see that they are not helpful in this situation. It is hard to solve math problems when you are tense, embarrassed, and frustrated. By focusing on her messy paper, other people's actions, and how she hates these tests, Jennifer is taking valuable time from solving any of the problems. If Jennifer continued to be upset and didn't do well on the remainder of the test, it could be an embarrassing experience. We don't know if she will ask for or receive help. It is possible that if she doesn't receive instruction in math or test-taking skills, she may lose confidence in her ability in math or math tests.

SELF-TALK #2 REVIEW

Feelings: We see that Jennifer gets upset, but quickly makes an effort to calm down. She does this by actually giving herself the instructions "calm down, slow down," and by refocusing her attention on ways to improve her situation.

Actions: Jennifer's actions include calming down and developing a strategy for the rest of the test. In addition, she plans her action (requesting help from her teacher) in case she does not succeed in solving the problem in the time allowed.

Results: We cannot be certain that Jennifer will make a better grade by using this self-talk, but using her time and energy to plan and find solutions probably will give her an edge. Damon Runyon once said,

> The race does not always go to the swift,
> The battle does not always go to the strong,
> . . . But that's the way to bet.
> "Runyon's Law"

Jennifer has increased her odds of doing better on the test by maintaining self-confidence and not developing negative feelings toward math and math tests.

Case Study 2: Meeting Adversity

Rosedale High School has the best football team among the public high schools in the county. For the past three years, however, Rosedale has lost in the district playoffs to Oldfield Academy, a private school in a nearby city.

In this year's playoff game Oldfield is leading once again. The score is 13–3, with five minutes remaining in the third quarter. John, a junior at Rosedale, is a guard on the offensive line. He is walking off the field after Oldfield has intercepted a pass and stopped a Rosedale drive.

Self-Talk #1: "What's the use? We can't beat these guys. They knock us out of the playoffs every year. It's not fair! These damn private schools recruit from all over the state. They give fat scholarships to the best athletes, and we only pick from people who live in our town.

"They should be in another division. Let them play bigger schools or only private schools. Why should I keep busting my rear end? What's the difference if I give up? We didn't have a chance to begin with."

Self-Talk #2: "Damn! We had a good drive going and we gave up the ball again. These guys are tough. They're a bunch of good athletes, but so are we. It's better to play good competition. It brings out the best in us and helps us improve and learn where we have to work harder. We can still beat them. I can dig deeper. This is my chance to push myself. I love the challenge. Come on, defense, get the ball back. I want another shot at these guys."

Case Study 3: Following the "Star" Brother

Mike is in his first year of junior high school. He is a fairly good student, but has never made the grades his brother Steve made. Steve, who graduated from junior high school last year, was one of the top students and the editor of the student newsletter.

Mrs. Pinkerton is the faculty advisor to the newsletter.

One day early in the school year she approaches Mike and says, "Michael, I'm so glad you started junior high this year. We really miss Steve, and it's good to have another fine student from your family. You know, I'm the advisor to the student newsletter, and I'd love to have you join our staff. Let me know if you're interested."

"Thank you for asking me," Mike responded. "I'll let you know pretty soon."

As Mike walks away, he thinks . . .

Self-Talk #1: "I knew it. Everybody is going to compare me with Steve and always expect me to do what he did. He's just a brain. I'm not. I can't write like he can. He can write about anything. I'm not going to join that dumb student newsletter. Who reads it anyway? Just the kids who write it and their parents. What a joke!"

Self-Talk #2: "Oh boy, I hope Mrs. Pinkerton isn't expecting me to be as smart as Steve. He aced everything when he was here. I do pretty good at school but I don't rack up the grades he does, and I wouldn't know the first thing about being editor. That's kind of silly thinking. Mrs. Pinkerton didn't ask me to be editor, she just invited me to join the group. I'm sure Steve didn't know everything about it when he started. It might be fun to try it. I kind of like to write and I'm sure they won't make me do a big story right away. The ninth graders probably do that and I'll bet Mrs. Pinkerton checks it out. I'll ask Steve what it was like and maybe I'll give it a try."

Case Study 4: Analyzing Losses

Terri has made the jump from the freshman girls' tennis team to the varsity team. She is ranked eighth at her school and has been competing in matches against other teams for the past two months. She has won some sets, but has yet to win a match. Today she lost another match. After winning the first set, she lost the second, and then her opponent came from behind to take the final set. As she takes her seat next to her teammates she thinks . . .

Self-Talk #1: "I never get the breaks! I can't believe this happens to me every time. I'm so much better than her it's ridiculous. I crushed her the first set. She doesn't even know how you're supposed to hit a backhand. All her shots fell in and mine were out by inches. I'm not even sure mine were really out.

"I'm jinxed. I have been ever since I made the team. I probably won't win a match all season because something always happens to make me lose."

Self-Talk #2: "This is so frustrating. I let another match get away. This happens over and over. I get ahead and then lose a close one. Now I've got no wins after four matches. I know my strokes are as good as or better than most of the girls I've played. I even hit better than some of the girls ahead of me on our team.

"Why do I blow leads and lose the close ones? I'm quick and I hit the ball hard, but I guess there's more to winning than that. There is something I need to improve. Is it my strategy and shot selection? Maybe I ease up when I'm ahead and lose concentration. Maybe it's the opposite. Maybe I try too hard and tense up.

"I'm going to take some time tonight and go over my matches to see if I can figure out where I need to get better. Then I'll ask the coach and Sandy for their advice. Sandy always seems to win the close matches."

Case Study 5: School Band Tryout

The elementary school band is made up of fourth-, fifth-, and sixth-graders. Joanne, who is in the fifth grade, has been studying the violin for two years. Last year she wanted to join the band but was afraid to try out.

After another year of lessons she felt a little more confident and signed up for the tryouts, which are scheduled for Thursday morning. On Wednesday evening she is thinking about the audition.

Self-Talk #1: "I never had an auditon before. I played before my teacher and my family but this is different. Mrs. Smith is going to judge me. What if I play badly? What if I get nervous and forget the music? I'll be so embarrassed. Everybody knows I tried out and they'll tease me. They'll say, 'Look at Joanne. She took lessons for two years and still couldn't get into the dinky school band.' "

Self-Talk #2: "I never had an audition before. I'll probably be a little nervous. My teacher says everybody gets butterflies, but they go away when you start to play and concentrate on the music. I've played this music so many times. I'm just going to imagine that I'm playing for my teacher and my Mom.

"If I make a mistake I'm not going to let it upset me. I'll just keep playing. Jane's in the band and she makes mistakes all the time. I'm sure Mrs. Smith wants people in the band who love music like I do."

Case Study 6: The Book Report

Mr. Brownwood, who teaches sophomore English at Lincoln High School, has assigned a book report on *Little Women*. The students must write their own reports, and each report must be at least eight pages long. The reports are assigned on a Monday and are due in two weeks.

Joshua is in Mr. Brownwood's class, and the following Saturday he is sitting at home thinking about the book report.

Self-Talk #1: "Why do I have to do this dumb report? *Little Women!* What does that have to do with anything? It was written ages ago, and I'm sure people thought it was sappy even then. Brownwood's brain is buried in those old novels. He ought to go 'back to the future' and stay there. I wish I was in Johnson's class.

"It's not due for another week. I've got basketball practice today and I want to go to the show tomorrow. I'll wait 'til next weekend. Suzie will have hers all done by then. She can tell me about it and I'll whip out a report on Sunday."

Self-Talk #2: "Wow, an eight-page report. That's at least 2,000 words! It's going to take me a couple of days just to read the book, and it's not my favorite sort of reading. I'd better make a plan to do this; it's just the kind of assignment I could put off until the last minute. It's always easy to put off the things you don't want to do.

"Well, it probably won't be too bad. It is a classic so there must be something good about it. A book report isn't too hard because you can pretty much say what's in the book and how you felt about it.

"I'm going to read it this weekend. I'll write the report during the week and then next weekend I won't have it hanging over my head."

REVIEW
Take a moment to review these case studies and the stories of Andrea and Jim in Chapter 1. What have you learned?

You are now ready to move on to deepen your understanding of the power of self-talk. You'll learn how your children can acquire helpful self-talk, positive mental habits, and useful performance skills.

CHAPTER 3

THE POWER OF SELF-TALK

REALISTIC POSITIVE STATEMENTS, REPEATED INWARDLY BY
THE CHILD, DETERMINE TO A LARGE EXTENT HIS GOOD
OPINION OF HIMSELF AND THE WORLD AROUND HIM.

HAIM GINOTT
Between Parent and Child

THE GREATEST DISCOVERY IN OUR GENERATION IS THAT
HUMAN BEINGS, BY CHANGING THE INNER ATTITUDES OF
THEIR MINDS, CAN CHANGE THE OUTER ASPECTS OF THEIR
LIVES.

WILLIAM JAMES
The Philosophy of William James

In these quotes, Ginott and James are focusing our attention
on some primary parental concerns:

How do our children talk to themselves?
What are their inner attitudes?
How can they acquire helpful self-messages?
Can they learn to change negative attitudes?

The case studies given in the last chapter provide some
answers. They reveal clearly three basic principles underly-
ing the methods and program presented in this book.

1. In any situation, there are alternative ways of reacting.
   Human beings can make choices about their thoughts
   and focus.
2. The choices we make and the self-talk we use can have

an immediate and important impact on our feelings and behavior.

3. Children, even preschoolers, can learn to use helpful self-talk and can change attitudes that work against their best interests.

These ideas seem logical, but as we react and respond to circumstances in our daily life, most of us aren't aware of choices and alternatives. Some of you might be saying to yourself: "I didn't *choose* to think that way; I just reacted automatically." Your experience is valid. We can make choices, but in practice we are often "on automatic." Because of the power of mental habits, we often don't make *conscious* choices.

UNDERSTANDING HABITS

Let's try some simple experiments. First fold your arms on your chest the way that feels most comfortable. Now fold your arms again, but reverse the top arm and the bottom arm.

Now unfold your arms, take a pen and paper, and sign your name the way you normally do. Then sign it again, but skip every other letter. This way requires only half the physical work, but it takes two or three times as long.

These quick experiences with habits can teach us a few things:

> Habits are comfortable.
> Habits are automatic; we don't have to think about them.
> Habits are not easy to change.
> We are not always aware of what habits we have.

How do these observations apply to our thoughts?

ATTITUDES ARE MENTAL HABITS

Like all habits, mental habits are learned and repeated, and they often become automatic. When we first learn to drive, for example, we are strongly aware of each movement, but after we've mastered the skills, we drive by habit. We act automatically and are not even aware of the steps involved unless we choose to notice them.

The same is true for our thoughts and attitudes. They are well formed and often repeated, and we tend not even to be aware of them. We don't think about what we think about. (Think about that!) We tend to respond automatically and to not notice how our thoughts contribute to our feelings. It's natural not to think of ourselves as choosing our thoughts because the habits and patterns are so strongly rooted. The thoughts just seem to happen, and we seem to have little control over them.

In some ways we are like the construction worker who sat down at noon and opened his lunch pail to find a peanut butter and jelly sandwich. He exploded, "I can't stand it. Every single day the same crummy lunch; peanut butter and jelly, peanut butter and jelly!" His buddy said, "Why don't you tell your wife to make something else?" "Oh, I make my own lunch," replied the first man.

LISTENING TO SELF-TALK
We all know that habits can be unlearned as well as learned, and I hope I've triggered your curiosity about your child's mental pattern as well as your own. If you are practical and result-oriented, you are probably wondering how your family can learn and change.

The magic key is self-talk. Self-talk is the key to awareness, to motivation for change, to self-mastery. We all talk to ourselves most of the time. Do you ever listen to your "mind chatter"? If you do, you notice immediately how rapidly your mind works. Research shows that normal conversation with another person is conducted at about 125 to 150 words per minute, but self-talk speeds on at rates of

400 to 600 words per minute: up to 10 words per second of instruction, criticism, comment, and dialogue with yourself.

Garbage in, Garbage out

What is the effect of all this self-talk? A useful starting point in our understanding is the analogy of the brain to a computer. Our 10 billion brain cells have often been described as a supercomputer, but (like all computers), they follow the law of GIGO: garbage in, garbage out. The computer doesn't say, "I know you didn't mean to program me this way. I'll change it around for you." It simply processes the program you read in.

Our brains work in the same way. In twenty years of working with individuals in all types of settings, I've found that children and adults—myself included—often say irrational, illogical, exaggerated, and unhelpful things to themselves and never question any of it.

Positive Programming

It may be helpful to consider that one of your goals as a parent is to provide positive programming for your child. Peers, teachers, media, and experiences will deliver a great deal of programming that will shape your child's mental habits, attitudes, and values. I'm inviting you to guide your child's inner development consciously and competently and to increase his or her chances for acquiring useful skills that will last a lifetime.

> *Teach a child to choose the right path and when he is older he will remain on it.* —Proverbs 22:6

Long before our children leave our homes for good, we accept the fact that we can't be there to guide them every moment. Every day they are in situations where they are on their own—choosing, deciding, and reacting. Teaching them helpful self-talk and showing them that they have the power to direct their thoughts is an essential positive ingredient in their growth.

Choosing our Focus

Not only do we have the ability to choose what we say to ourselves; we also can select what we *focus* on in a situation. Focus strongly influences how we think, feel, and eventually act.

In *Zen and the Art of Motorcycle Maintenance*, Robert Pirsig says about focus, "We take a handful of sand from the endless landscapes of awareness around us and call that handful of sand the world."

As this quote suggests, we select our focus but are almost never aware of our choice or of the possible alternative choices. Our focus shapes our awareness and our consciousness. No one else can choose the contents of our mind; we must be the ones to make these choices. Yet in daily life we tend not to see how important focus is in determining how we feel and react. We tend to be unaware that we are focusing on some aspects of our environment and not on others.

Taking charge of our focus is a key to directing our inner lives. We can see or read about dramatic examples of this ability. Mother Teresa cares for the sick and dying in the Calcutta slums. When questioned about her motivation in caring for diseased and hopeless people, she replied that she envisions each one of them as the body of her Saviour. In another area, many of us saw Mary Lou Retton's perfect vault in the 1984 Summer Olympics, which earned her the gold medal. Imagine the single-minded focus she attained while knowing that almost a billion people were watching her and that even a score of 9.95 would not win the gold.

These are notable examples of two individuals who

control their inner lives. I'm not guaranteeing that your children will achieve such mastery through this book, but Mother Teresa and Mary Lou Retton did start somewhere. At some point in their lives they learned that they could take charge of their focus.

To increase your awareness, I've listed below the differences in focus between Self-Talk #1 and Self-Talk #2 in each case study in Chapter 2. Note the effects of these differences.

Where Is the Focus?

Case Study 1: The Fourth-Grade Math Test

Self-Talk #1

> What she can't do
> Other people's success
> Her messy paper
> Other people seeing her erase

Self-Talk #2

> Calming down
> Test-taking strategy
> Solutions
> Learning

Case Study 2: Meeting Adversity

Self-Talk #1

> Unfairness
> Changing the divisions
> Chances of losing
> Quitting

Self-Talk #2

> Positive aspects of his team and the other team
> Positive aspects of competition
> Chances of winning
> Playing

Case Study 3: Following the "Star" Brother

Self Talk #1

> What Steve can do
> What Mike can't do
> Negative aspects of the student newsletter

Self-Talk #2

> What Steve can do
> How Mike compares with Steve
> Realistic expectations
> Positive aspects of joining the newsletter staff

Case Study 4: Analyzing Losses

Self-Talk #1

> Why she should have won
> Luck
> Negative expectations

Self-Talk #2

> Losses
> Assessment of factors
> Learning and asking for help

Case Study 5: School Band Tryout

Self-Talk #1

Negative results
Being teased and feeling embarrassed

Self-Talk #2

Coping with nervousness
Previous success
Handling mistakes
Positive feelings about Mrs. Smith

Case Study 6: The Book Report

Self-Talk #1

Negative aspects of the book
How he could postpone writing the report

Self-Talk #2

Realistic assessment of time needed
Positive reasons for doing the assignment
Action plan

We will return to the subject of focus at several points in later chapters. Learning to shift focus helps many children reduce or eliminate the excessive pressure they feel in a variety of situations.

GENERAL GUIDELINES FOR TEACHING SELF-TALK
In this chapter and those that follow, you will note some specific examples of self-talk and attitudes that would be beneficial for your child to acquire. Here are some general guidelines to help you teach self-talk.

1. Learn it before you teach it.
Modeling is more effective than preaching.

2. Don't teach the whole idea all at once; introduce the ideas slowly.

3. Look for the "teachable" moment.
Avoid trying to teach self-talk when your child is upset. Teachable moments often occur when there is no performance going on. Relaxed conversations are excellent times, especially if they concern some activity your child wants to pursue. Talking about his or her heroes also creates many opportunities for planting the seeds of ideas.

4. Don't teach all the time.
Try to space and balance your comments. You will be amazed at how many opportunities you will have to instill values and attitudes. Most parents have hundreds each year—perhaps a thousand if you spend a lot of time with your child.

Also, it's usually best to use a variety of sources in addition to direct teaching, such as modeling, stories, television, movies, newspaper articles, teachers, other parents, coaches, or other children.

5. Don't just talk; listen.
When a child (or an adult) is upset or has strong feelings, confrontation with a logical argument from your point of view isn't always effective. Often it is better to listen effectively. Try to understand what the child is saying based on his inner world. You will learn how he thinks and feels. Even if he doesn't have the whole truth, he probably has a piece of it that may be important for you to know.

One father told me that one day while practicing, his

seven-year-old started to lose confidence in his soccer abilities. The father tried to reassure him that he was a good player and was kicking the ball well, but his son grew more and more upset. Finally the father just listened. What emerged, accompanied by many tears, was, "If I'm not a great soccer player you won't love me." The father insisted, "No, I love you no matter what you do in a game." The boy replied, "But you would love me more if I'm good at soccer."

The boy had grasped a truth about their relationship. Unintentionally, the father had placed a great emphasis on soccer performance, which put a lot of pressure on his son. He hugged the boy and didn't say much more that afternoon, but afterward he made a conscious effort to pay attention to a variety of his son's activities.

CHAPTER 4

LEARNING TO LEARN

WHAT ANY PERSON IN THE WORLD CAN LEARN, ALMOST
ALL PERSONS CAN LEARN IF PROVIDED WITH APPROPRIATE
PRIOR AND CURRENT CONDITIONS OF LEARNING.

DR. BENJAMIN BLOOM
Developing Talent in Young People

IF YOU CAN LEARN TO LEARN FROM FAILURE, YOU'LL GO
PRETTY MUCH WHERE YOU WANT TO GO.

ARTHUR GORDON
On the Far Side of Failure

ACHIEVEMENT AND LEARNING

Owen B. Butler, the former chief executive officer of
Procter and Gamble, directed a sixty-member panel that
investigated U.S. educational systems. The panel's report,
"Investing in our Children: Business and the Public
Schools" (1985), emphasized the concern that our children
might be unprepared for the challenges of the future and
stressed that schools should focus on teaching the skills of
"learning how to learn."

Business leaders are trying to pinpoint educational needs
for two major reasons. First, businesses have spent almost
$40 billion to train and reeducate employees. Second,
many American industries are competing for survival with
overseas companies, particularly Japanese. The fact that
Japanese students go to school until 5 P.M. each day and

also attend on Saturdays seems to make that competiton even keener.

With good reason, then, business people, political leaders, educators, and parents all want to transform our children into lifelong learners. A 1978 *Family Circle* study traced the backgrounds of 50 highly successful Americans and found that in each home there was an effort to communicate a zest for learning. Similarly, an investigation by Victor, Mildred, and Ted. G. Goertzel of 400 people who were eminent in their fields found parental emphasis on love of learning.

More recently, Charles Garfield, Ph.D., has published his research on peak performance in a book entitled *Peak Performance*. After interviewing 1600 achievers, he found that peak performers share, among other qualities, confidence in their capacity to learn and the mental agility to respond to change.

How do we develop that kind of learner? We can start by looking at examples of learners, the specific characteristics of a learner, and detailed methods and suggestions that will help us help our children to acquire these qualities.

THE ATTITUDE OF A LEARNER

In addition to encouraging achievement and growth, the attitude of a learner is the best available antidote to excessive pressure. Learners have a built-in pressure inoculation that helps them keep the stress of performance at a manageable level. They've taken the sting out of failure by accepting mistakes and less-than-perfect performance as they learn.

Indeed, a key quality of learners is moving toward goals and shaking off mistakes and setbacks by learning from them but not overemphasizing them. In his book *Actualizations*, Stewart Emery stresses this attitude of a learner. One of his most striking models is a baby who is learning how to walk. As she falls and tries again, her brain, nervous system, and muscles are learning. They baby doesn't count the spills as mistakes or failures. She simply focuses on her goal of walking, which she eventually achieves.

Fortunately a baby doesn't have some of our self-talk; if she did, she might never learn to walk:

> "I fell down again; that's the tenth time today. I'm terrible at this. I'll never learn to walk."
> "I'm a year old now and I still can't walk. My sister walked when she was 10 months old; what's wrong with me?"

Thomas Edison is an excellent example of the persistence and productivity of a lifelong learner. He left us more than three million pages of notes, and his famous efforts to invent the light bulb involved over 6,000 experiments. When questioned about all these failures he replied, "Nonsense, I learned 6,000 ways not to invent the light bulb."

The case studies you've read in Chapters 1 and 2 also provide examples of the attitude of a learner:

> Andrea, asking for help from her teacher and cousin Jim.
> Jim, honestly evaluating his performance and thinking about how to improve on last-second shots.
> John, wanting to play tough competition so he could improve.
> Mike, realistic about being a beginner, and willing to join the student newsletter.
> Terri, taking an honest look at why she loses the close matches and deciding to ask for feedback and coaching.
> Joanne, with a sensible attitude toward mistakes.
> Joshua, focusing on the positive reasons for reading *Little Women* and completing the assigned report.

These examples highlight different aspects of a learner's attitude. Specific characteristics mark the learner, and as you read about them you will see why children who possess them won't easily be derailed from developing their talents and potential.

CHARACTERISTICS OF A LEARNER

Curiosity

Eleanor Roosevelt once remarked, "I think that at a child's birth, if a mother could ask a fairy godmother to endow it with the most useful gift, that gift would be curiosity." Human beings survive and thrive as individuals and as a species by learning from their environment. We are "wired" to learn from birth. Learning is as natural as breathing when we are infants, and lifelong learners retain a special excitement about new information and skills.

Optimism

Rene Dubos, a world-renowned scientist, coined the phrase "Trend is not destiny," which could serve as the motto of learners. In *Celebrations of Life* he cites many examples of how human beings become aware of negative trends and use their ingenuity and inventiveness to reverse them.

Confidence in one's capacity to learn generates hope, "the passion for the possible." Learners are realistic, but their realistic assessments tend to include the possibilities of growth, learning, and change.

In a sense, learners have discovered the fountain of youth. As long as they keep learning about their problems, discovering new information, and acquiring new skills, freshness and optimism abound.

Positive Attitude toward Mistakes

Learners don't *want* to make mistakes, but they have a realistic, accepting attitude about the inevitability of making them. Mistakes and setbacks are an unavoidable part of living, and they tend to crop up when we acquire new skills and tackle new ventures. Thomas J. Watson, former president of IBM, advised:

> *You can be discouraged by failure—or you can learn from it. So go ahead and make mistakes. Make all you can. Because remember, that's where you'll find success. On the far side of failure.*

In the self-talk and teaching suggestions sections in this chapter, I stress the importance of this attitude for children. They can easily be discouraged and develop the fear of failure. In *The Absorbent Mind*, Maria Montessori writes on this subject, "If a child is to stop making mistakes, he must become more skillful, and how can he do this if, being already below standard, he is also discouraged?"

Learners have the "courage to be imperfect" (Rudolph Dreikurs, author of *Children, The Challenge*) and the wisdom to convert mistakes into lessons.

MISTAKES = LESSONS

Openness to Feedback

Stewart Emery *(Actualizations)* finds that people differ in their desire for *protection* or *correction*. Learners seek out and are open to correction. They want helpful feedback in the areas they need to improve. Many people, however, would rather have protection. When I'm called in as an organizational consultant to a company, I often ask people, "What do you do around here when you make a mistake?" Unfortunately, the reply is often, "Don't tell anybody."

Confucius said, "A man who commits a mistake and doesn't admit it is committing another mistake." The learner is willing to admit mistakes and ask for help, and often sets up systems to obtain feedback and new information about his performance. Usually the best performers want the most information, and those who need it most avoid it.

John Moore, a sales manager of resort properties in the Pocono Mountains of Pennsylvania, relates an example:

> I decided to provide a training seminar for my sales team, but I couldn't let everyone go through it at once. Since there were a number of people who were performing at a mediocre or marginal level, I decided to let these people attend the seminar first. My top performers would go through the training later. After I made this announcement I got two types of complaints. The poorer performers complained that they had to go to a seminar and the top salespeople complained because they couldn't get the training right away.

Having protection as a goal is like running around your backhand in tennis. You can win some matches but your backhand won't improve. Learners are willing to pay the price; they'll hit their backhand into the net or off the court and even lose some matches because they know they will improve.

PROTECTION vs. CORRECTION

Willingness to Take Risks

Sometimes children's fear of failure is clearly visible, as in the case of the seven-year-old I discussed in the Introduction who was desperate to get all the block designs right. Much more often, though, the fear of failure is undetected because the child *avoids any chance of failure.* One form this fear takes is not trying an activity at all. Another is doing it with a half-hearted effort, which allows the child to say, "I didn't really even try."

I refer to this nontrying, nonrisking behavior as *hidden protectionism.* The child's standards of success and lack of confidence combine to say, "I'll fail, I'll be mediocre, I won't be good enough." Almost all parents have struggled through this conversation:

"Honey, why don't you try it?"
"I can't do it."
"How do you know you can't do it if you don't even try it?"
"I know I can't do it."

Maybe we've heard, "It's dumb" or "I don't like it." Often these statements really mean, "I want to do it but I'm afraid I won't be any good at it. I don't want to be embarrassed."

Learners are more willing to take risks. They can overcome the fear of failure because emotionally they are able to reduce the sting of failure.

STING OF FAILURE ⟶ FEAR OF FAILURE

Goal Oriented

Learners keep track of accomplishments, not failures. The first store that J. C. Penney opened went broke, but he opened over a thousand more.

It's very hard to stop learners because they use their time and energy to pursue their goals persistently. They suffer setbacks and detours, but these don't become the focus of their attention.

TIME AND ENERGY ⟶ GOALS

Ability to Learn from Successes

While many people simply celebrate successes, learners take the extra time to analyze them. They know that they can often learn much more by crystallizing and clarifying in their minds exactly what they did right.

How come I kicked the ball so well that time?
Why did that play work?
What were my study habits for that test?
Why did my sister and I get along so well this afternoon?

Resourcefulness in Problem Solving

A familiar saying goes: "If you give a man a fish he can eat for a day, but if you teach a man to fish he can eat for a lifetime." Resourcefulness is the ability to figure out what to do *when there are no more fish left*.

Learners accept that they must continue to learn and adapt. If life temporarily doesn't provide problems and challenges, they create their own by raising their standards. By confronting adversity or self-created challenges they develop their own resourcefulness as well as their confidence to cope with change. These characteristics—resourcefulness and confidence—add up to the attitude of a learner. I've never met anyone who exhibits them in all areas of their life, but they are worthy goals.

The Self-Talk of a Learner

The attitude of a learner, like all mental habits, can be broken down into specific self-talk and reactions. Following are examples of the self-talk associated with the learner's attitude.

> I can learn and improve.
> I love to learn and get better.
> If I stick with it, I'll get it.
> It's just an error, get back on track.
> Mistakes are part of learning. I'm going to turn this mistake into a lesson.
> How can I improve?
> What did I do right that I want to repeat?
> I'm just starting. Of course I'm going to make errors.
> It doesn't have to be perfect.
> What can I learn from what happened?
> Everybody makes mistakes, even Mom and Dad.
> How can I prevent this from happening again?
> Oops, I made a mistake. Good thing I checked. Now I'd better correct it and be more careful.
> My parents and my teachers want to help me learn. I can ask them for help.
> It's okay to admit I don't know and ask someone who does.

I'm getting better!
I'm learning!
I got it!
I can't get any better unless I try it.
If I practice and get coaching I'll learn it.
I can turn it around.
I can learn what I need to learn.

METHODS AND TEACHING SUGGESTIONS

How do we nurture the attitude of a learner? Language is an excellent method. Language helps to guide and regulate a child. Words signal when to stop or start behavior, and parents have this verbal control in the first years of the child's life. Gradually, children learn to use language to control themselves. Preschoolers regularly talk out loud to themselves as a way of guiding their actions, especially when they are learning or doing something new.

By first grade most of this spoken control has been replaced by inner speech, which serves the same functions of self-guidance, self-regulation, and self-control. This inner speech—self-talk—will be our focus.

Although the methods I describe can be applied to children three years old and up, infants can understand and absorb language, so the pattern of language to encourage positive self-talk should be laid down early.

I now invite you to take the attitude of a learner about parenting and tackle the self-talk methods and suggestions that follow.

1. Use key words early and often.
   When talking to youngsters, even two- and three-year-olds, introduce the words that you hope will be part of their inner environment: *learn, improve, get better, practice, try.*

2. Convey your enthusiasm and approval about your child's learning and progress.

Children need to know that learning is one of your important values. It helps them feel your excitement about their growth and mastery.

3. Focus on the right way of doing things, and the mistakes will often disappear.

When a child is learning how to hit a baseball, do long division, or spell, he or she often improves even though little attention is paid to mistakes. If you concentrate on making clear the correct way of doing it, the mistakes often disappear by themselves. (See Chapter 6.)

4. Determine what kind of mistake has been made.

Is it a mistake that occurred because of a lack of skill (a "can do" problem) or because of a lack of effort (a "will do" problem)?

"Can do" errors occur because the child isn't skillful enough or because there are obstacles blocking the desired action. It is very important to understand *why* something happened.

"Could she reach it?"
"Can he open that jar?"
"Is it too heavy or too full?"
"Does she have an alarm clock?"
"Is there enough time to do the chores and be ready?"
"Does he know exactly what he is expected to do and when?"
"Could we set up reminders?"

Often we get upset or punish children for mistakes or poor performance because we've misjudged their ability or the support they need to do it correctly. If there are real obstacles, if the instructions weren't clear, or if the child needs more coaching or support, we need to focus our attention and energy on those aspects. At other times, poor performance or mistakes are really "will do" problems. The child is not making the effort. In these situations the child could do the task and do it correctly if he or she was willing.

Try to sort out the "can do" and the "will do" factors that are affecting your child's performance.

5. Emphasize practice, effort, and growth, not genetics.
Children are often unaware of skill acquisition unless we point it out to them. When they see talented youngsters or adults they sometimes conclude that people are born athletes or scholars. This conclusion is a dangerous myth, and it is important to present evidence and examples that contradict this way of thinking.

6. Use their heroes as examples.
Often children don't realize that their heroes are learners. I was trying to explain the importance of learning to my son, then seven years old, when he asked me, "What if you know everything already?" He mentioned the baseball player Pete Rose, whom he had seen break Ty Cobb's record for lifetime hits a few weeks before.

When I told him that Pete Rose, even at his age, works on his game and is always looking for an edge, my son looked surprised. Then he broke into a big grin.

7. Read stories about people who made an effort to learn.
Dr. Spencer Johnson wrote an inspiring series of books, *Value Tales*, about the lives of famous people. Many of these books illustrate the attitude and values of the learner. Madame Curie's total dedication to research, for example, made her the only person ever to win the Nobel Prize in both physics and chemistry.

8. Make your child aware of his or her progress and improvement.

When your child does master an activity or task, you can recognize it and also use it as an opportunity to reinforce some ideas about learning.

> "See, you stuck with it and didn't give up, and now you can do it."
>
> "Remember when you thought you would never learn it? Now look at you!"
>
> "You said, 'I can't do it,' and didn't even want to try. Now you see why I wanted you to try it. You're doing well and now you like it."
>
> "It feels great to improve, doesn't it? Doesn't it give you the confidence to tackle other things?"

9. Learn to forgive them so they can forgive themselves.

In addition to appreciating children's accomplishments, it's important to show forgiveness about their shortcomings. Remember, self-esteem derives from acceptance as well as achievement, and children need to know that your love is more enduring than their latest performance.

The impact of an act of forgiveness can last a lifetime. In *How to Live Every Day of Your Life*, Margaret Johnstone relates this story about financier Bernard Baruch:

> He once persuaded his father to invest in an overhead trolley line that ran between the landing and a hotel at Put-in-Bay in Lake Erie. His father invested $8,000, a considerable part of his life savings, and every cent was lost.
>
> Baruch says, "Although my father never reproached me, the loss weighed on my heart. I imagine I took the matter harder than my father, who was more concerned with human values than with money."
>
> Some time after this fiasco, Baruch mentioned to his

mother that if he had $500 he could make some money in
another investment. She suggested that he ask his father,
but he said "never" after the Put-in-Bay disaster. A few
days later, Baruch's father came to him with a check for
$500.

Says Bernard Baruch, "The profound lift it was to my
self-respect to learn that after I had cost him so much, my
father still had faith in me. . . ."

In his autobiography Baruch recalls the day early in this century when he achieved a net worth of a million dollars. The first person he told was his father.

This story has a special meaning to me because I, too, talked my father into joining me in an investment that went sour. I expected him to be angry with me when I told him what had happened. Instead he sat with me and told me about some bad money decisions he had made, and he said he hoped I had learned something about investing from this loss.

There is a particular kind of love that we can feel only when we have failed and are still loved. It doesn't make us love failure; it helps us love ourselves and gives us the courage to try again.

MODELING

Although the teaching suggestions just outlined are excellent methods for instilling in your child a learner's attitude, the most powerful teaching method you have is your own action. Psychologists have long recognized that most human behavior is acquired through "observational learning."

Dr. Paul Kienel, president of the Association of Christian Schools International, states, "Your children are watching you, whether you realize it or not. They are observing your every move. They are learning more from you than all their teachers, preachers, and peers combined."

You can use this power of modeling to deliver a living performance that conveys the messages you want to send more effectively than any lecture. Here are some specific actions that will make you a model of a learner and influence your child's attitudes and actions.

1. **Get excited about learning new things.**
   No matter what your age, you can learn at work and in your relationships, hobbies, leisure, and personal health care. As you read this book you are learning about yourself, parenting, self-talk, and children. The major goal is to show your children that you continue to learn and grow and that it's great to be able to increase your knowledge and ability.

2. **Tell your children about the mistakes you've made and continue to make.**
   I'm not suggesting that you pull all your skeletons out of the closet if that would overwhelm or frighten your child. I'm referring to the normal errors in judgment and memory and the lapses in effort and ability that occur in all our lives. If children view you as perfect and infallible, they have more trouble being realistic about their own mistakes and shortcomings.

3. **Be a self-accepting learner.**
   When you make a mistake, try to talk about it with some self-acceptance. Put the major focus on learning from the mistake and correcting it, rather than calling yourself bad names. Try saying, "That new bread recipe didn't turn out too well, did it? That's disappointing. But it was my first try. Let me go over the recipe and figure out why it didn't rise and is so dry," instead of, "That bread is so awful. I'm so sorry. Don't eat it. The recipe is so simple. What's wrong with me? I just can't bake my own bread and I never will. That's the last time I try that."

Use the self-accepting and self-correcting approach to everyday errors and events. You will show that you are concerned about doing things correctly, but that you emphasize improving yourself rather than putting yourself down.

4. Demonstrate your openness to feedback.
If you are acquiring new skills, show or explain to your child how feedback is helping you improve.

Feedback comes in many forms, but it always contains information that we need but would not get otherwise. We can receive feedback from charts, scales, a basketball hoop, math tests, mirrors, videotaping, recording our voices, questionnaires, surveys, friends, peers, supervisors, children, dogs, customers, blood pressure tests, and computers.

I'm not suggesting that you believe everything anyone says to you. Feedback needs to be filtered and analyzed. Even so, you can make an indelible impression on your children by asking for their feedback about cooking, tennis, or parenting, and using some of that information to improve.

5. Do some things you're not good at.
It's great for little Suzie to see that Mom and Dad are poor or mediocre at some things but try them anyway. If you're a good sport, you and your family can have a healthy laugh together.

By restricting your efforts only to the activities you excel at, you prevent your child from seeing you as a learner. You also rob him or her of the pleasure of mastering a dance routine while you stumble around, or of whizzing down a ski slope while two instructors are trying to pull you out of a snow bank. Reinforce your attitude by announcing, "Well, I can't get any better at it if I don't try it."

6. Ask for help sometimes.

It's amazing how many children and adults learn not to ask for help or admit they don't know something. In business I encounter this problem frequently, even with people in highly responsible positions. It's obviously not helpful for an adult, but it can be devastating for a child who needs assistance in so many areas.

You can demonstrate the naturalness of needing and asking for help in a variety of ways:

> "Let's stop in that gas station and ask for directions."
> "I'm not sure I remember exactly how to go, so be sure to bring the map."
> "You know, Aunt Sally started her own business. I'm going to ask her about record keeping."
> "Tommy, I'd like your opinion on this."
> "I need your help with this."

If you ask your children for help and receive it, you give them the bonus of being meaningful contributors to your life. I'm not suggesting that you burden them with most of your problems and responsibilities; just ask yourself occasionally, "Am I letting them help me? Am I needing them, too?"

7. Focus on solutions.

Problems provide learning opportunities for you and your child. While you are learning how to solve a problem, children can learn about your problem-solving attitudes and strategies. Naturally they will see you upset; no one wants problems. But how long do you stay upset? When do you start focusing on solutions? How quickly do you move from *stewing* to *doing?*

You can improve your approach to problem solving

and teach useful self-talk by adopting "solution consciousness." Try to use these phrases in front of your children:

> "Well, it happened. I'm upset, but now we have to deal with it."
> "What can I do now?"
> "What can we salvage out of this?"
> "Let's see why it happened."
> "What can I learn from this?"
> "How can I prevent this from happening again?"

This learning and solution-seeking approach to problems will gradually become part of your children's self-talk.

8. Use the learner's self-talk.

As you study the self-talk examples earlier in this chapter, add other phrases that strike a responsive chord with you. Then use these words in front of your child. Talk aloud occasionally before, during, and after activities. Let phrases like these sprinkle your conversation:

> "I just need to try this again. Then I'll get it."
> "Oops, I blew that one. Let's do it over and get back on track."
> "I'm stuck. I need to do more research or ask someone about it."
> "Hey, I'm getting it."
> "I need some feedback. I'm not sure what I'm doing right and what I'm doing wrong."
> "I did it!"

As we all know, the key to developing habits is repetition. In *Raising Good Children* Dr. Thomas Lickona advises:

> *I believe in telling kids what you think is important, what you think can help them in their lives. You have to*

catch them at the right time, and you can never be sure what that is. You may have to say it a lot before they start taking it in. But they'll remember it. They'll say, "My mother used to say. . . ."

REVIEW

Before moving on to other subjects, take a moment to review and note what is relevant and important to *you* about the attitude of a learner. Answering questions such as the following will help you set priorities and plan actions for your family:

What are the self-talk attitudes you need to learn?

What are the self-talk attitudes your child(ren) need(s) to learn?

What are the specific actions you will take?

CHAPTER 5

IDENTIFYING STRENGTHS AND POTENTIAL

KEEP AWAY FROM PEOPLE WHO TRY TO BELITTLE YOUR AMBITIONS. SMALL PEOPLE ALWAYS DO THAT, BUT THE REALLY GREAT MAKE YOU FEEL THAT YOU, TOO, CAN BECOME GREAT.

MARK TWAIN

One of the greatest gifts you can give to your children is your ability to recognize their ability. Children need a realistic, positive understanding of their strengths and potentials. Their self-talk should include:

"I can do . . ."
"I'm good at . . ."
"I could be really great at . . ."
"I have talent for . . ."
"I'm a good . . ."
"Some of the best things about me are . . ."
"If I really work hard I could become . . ."
"My parents and teachers think I could . . ."

This kind of self-talk begins and maintains the achievement cycle. The saying "an ounce of prevention is worth more than a pound of cure" certainly applies to children and their self-image. They will form many of their ideas about what their abilities do in their own family settings.

In the early 1960s Dr. Herbert Otto, a professor of social work at the University of Utah, was launching a study of problem families. The study involved taping family dinner conversations and then listening to the communication patterns. Like any good researcher, Otto needed a control group. In this case the control group consisted of average families with no serious marital, financial, or child problems.

What Otto discovered about these so-called average families surprised and interested him so much that he changed the entire direction of his career and founded the National Center for Exploration of Human Potential, in La Jolla, California. When he analyzed the tapes he learned that seventy-five percent of all the communication in these families was negative. The emphasis on putdowns, criticism, and conflict and the relative lack of positive, encouraging comments in these homes became the focal point of his life work. Further research confirmed his original findings and led him to conclude that very few people in our society are ever trained to identify and talk about the strengths, resources, and positive potential in others or in themselves. Most of us are more aware of faults and shortcomings.

Few qualities are more useful for your role as a spouse, parent, friend, or boss than the skill of seeing the good in people and telling them about it in a way they can believe.

By learning to communicate effectively to your children about their strengths and potential, you can achieve these things:

> Help them to reduce their negative self-focus and to put their strengths in proper perspective.
>
> Provide new insights about directions they can pursue successfully.
>
> Expand their self-image and build confidence.

Increase their motivation to improve, persist, and overcome obstacles.

Build a closer, trusting relationship.

Increase their openness to hearing constructive criticism from you.

Help them develop their ability to encourage and support siblings, friends, cousins, teammates, and even you.

Make yourself more aware of your own assets and good qualities.

NEGATIVE LABELS AND LIMITING BELIEFS

Young children are extremely suggestible. Pascal noted this when he said, "Man is so made that by continually telling him he is a fool, he believes it, and by continually telling it to himself he makes himself believe it."

Unfortunately, when children are called names or given negative labels, they often accept them as true. Some children struggle against the image, but doubts about themselves invariably arise. "Lazy," "selfish," "stupid," "irresponsible," "clumsy," "no good," "fat," "sloppy," "never be good at _____ ," "slow," "plain," "uncoordinated," "ugly"—these labels become limiting beliefs because they initiate and fuel the underachievement cycle.

Here are two strong recommendations for preventing this cycle.

1. Avoid using negative labels and calling your children names.

It's important to correct problem behavior, but this can be done without turning mistakes into faults.

The most damaging labels are those with a "genetic" element: "You're just like your father, lazy as can be." "Oh, honey, you're just like me. I could never do math either. It doesn't matter—you'll be popular." "Your grandfather had the same mischievous temperament. You always get in trouble like he did."

How can a child argue with heredity? It becomes a part of his or her self-concept that is hard to deny or eliminate. (In Chapter 8, "Building Responsibility and Self-Discipline," I describe specific techniques for improving performance without labeling a child.)

2. Learn to recognize, appreciate, and acknowledge a child's strengths on a regular basis.
(You will learn the techniques and skills for doing this effectively later in this chapter.) Although you may regret some of the things you've said and feel remiss about some things you haven't said to your children, don't be discouraged. You have an opportunity to do things differently, and negative self-image can change at any age. I learned this early in my career.

From 1972 to 1975 I had the good fortune to work with Dr. Otto at his institute in La Jolla, California. During the summers we trained teachers, counselors, and clergy in some of the strength-acknowledgment methods you are about to learn.

One summer a professor and his wife, Nancy, attended the sessions. For the first two days he was in Dr. Otto's group and she was in mine. As I began my session, Nancy remarked, "I guess this is the 'stupid' group." She explained that her husband was a brilliant professor, while she had dropped out of college thirty years earlier to become a mother. She concluded that her husband was in the advanced group with Dr. Otto, where she didn't belong. As the group got to know Nancy, she told us about her feelings of inferiority and, toward the end of the session, about her secret dream to return to school and become a counselor.

During the following two weeks, Nancy learned about her strengths and potential. She left California believing that she had something to offer people; that September, at the age of fifty, she went back to college. She earned her master's degree in counseling when she was fifty-three, and in addition to establishing a private practice she initiated women's self-help groups through her church.

Nancy went on to train other women to lead positive-focused groups, and designed a format for women like herself. Working through the structures and networks of their religious denomination, these groups reached hundreds of thousands of women. Not bad for a woman who thought she belonged in the "stupid" group!

Children can change their self-perception more rapidly. Positive feedback, a small success, or the discovery of a new talent can spark a new vision of what is attainable. "Losers" and "dummies" can shed their skins if they start to believe they have strengths, even small ones, to build upon.

THE STRENGTH-ACKNOWLEDGMENT METHOD

Otto's method can be used in families, groups, or work teams. Each person, in turn, receives the group's undivided attention, focusing exclusively on that person's talents, strengths, good qualities, and potentialities. This activity can help your whole family to acquire the skills of spotting strengths in other people and telling them about it. It can add to each family member's positive self-image and widen their perspective on how they can use their talents and gifts.

Guidelines

Here is a format, with guidelines and suggestions:

1. Explain why you are getting together.
   You might say, "Lots of times in our family we tell each other when we do things wrong but we don't always let

the other person know what they are doing right. Let's take the time to look at what we are doing well, what we are good at, and maybe even tell each other what we think the other one could be good at if they really wanted to."

2. Brainstorm about strengths.
"Before we talk about each one's strength, let's learn more about them. Let's make a list of things that could be good about people, and also things people are good at doing."

There are various ways to lead this activity, but it is a very important step. If you omit it, family members will be unsure about what a strength is and will be hesitant to share. Make sure they know that this list is about people in general, not any one person in the family. You might present categories to spark thinking:

School
Sports
Creative/artistic activities
Family life
Friendship
Work/chores
Hobbies

You might present a list of strengths to discuss and add to it:

Energy	Adaptable
Drive	Open
Idealism	Honest
Courage	Loyal
Independence	Sense of humor
Sense of justice	Optimistic
Fair	Positive outlook
Flexible	Serious

Sensitive to others' feelings	"Stick-to-it"-iveness
Kind	Dependable
Spontaneous	Enthusiastic
Fun-loving	Faithful
Playful	Good listener
Caring	Knowledgeable
Helpful	Organized
Creative	Self-esteem
Imaginative	Loving
Strong	Nice to animals
Coordinated	Helpful
Smart	Encourages people
Good cook	Runs fast
Responsible	Good memory
Disciplined	Shares things
Friendly	Good at tennis
Tries hard	Good at soccer
Good study habits	Good at gymnastics
Affectionate	Good at piano
Good character	Good at writing or drawing

3. Reduce "discounting."

At this point, many children and adults wonder whether they really have a strength. If these questions aren't answered they may "discount" or belittle their strengths and deny that they have them. A discussion of discounting habits can have as much impact on a child as actually hearing the family's view of his or her strengths. Use family discussion and/or your input to cover these ideas about discounting strengths.

These are the most common ways of discounting that need to be discussed before you start strength acknowledgment:

Not 100 percent: "I'm not that way all the time." A

person can have a strength even though it isn't used or acted on all the time. If you hear about a strength someone sees in you, don't deny it just because you can think of times when you weren't that way. Accept this strength and try to build on it.

Someone else is better: "Johnny is much better at that than I am." There will always be people who are better than you at some things. Sometimes when you see how good they are you get discouraged and don't see your own talents. Try to make it your goal to see your strengths and develop them. Remember, you definitely, positively can have a strength even if someone is better at it than you.

Too much: "I know I'm that way [for example, serious], but I'm too much that way." Some people feel they overuse their strengths. If you think you do, and you want to develop other parts of your personality or character, go ahead. But don't hate your strengths—don't "throw the baby out with the bath water"—your strengths are still important.

Someone doesn't think so: "But Mary doesn't think I'm smart." If someone else doesn't think you have a good quality, it can make you doubt whether you do. But don't let one person's opinion decide such an important matter. What do other people think? What do you really think about yourself? Try sincerely to give the people who think you have a strength as much credit as those who don't.

It's easy: "That's not a real strength, it's just easy for me." You are fortunate to have developed this talent or ability so easily. Many people struggle in this area, but you are gifted. Don't take these qualities for granted. These are important talents you can build on and develop further.

Born that way: "That's God-given. I didn't earn it." Through your genes, your environment, and your own efforts you have certain strengths and resources. Perhaps you feel that you have no special claim to some of your assets because they are God-given and you haven't worked hard to develop them. It may be helpful to acknowledge that you do possess them and find ways to use them that will benefit yourself and others.

4. **Give instructions to the family.**
"Everybody in our family will get a chance to hear about their strengths and what we like about them. Each one of us will take turns. When it's your turn you get to tell us what you think your strengths and good points are, and then we will tell you what we see. I'll write down what everyone says about you so you can remember it.

"When it's your turn, try to listen and be open to what people say to you. Remember, we may see a strength in you that is in its early stages but we still want to point it out. We will be giving our opinions and you can make up your mind about the ideas we share.

"When it's not your turn, concentrate on the person whose turn it is. Imagine that you're putting on special glasses that let you see their strengths and possibilities. Use your hunches. Be sure to mention anything the person did or accomplished that fit in with your ideas about them.

"It's okay to agree with other people or with the person whose turn it is. Sometimes your extra comment will help to convince that person that he or she actually has that strength.

"If you talk about a person's potential, mention what you think he or she *could* do with his strengths, not what he *should* do. This will make it easier for him to hear without feeling pressure."

These are some typical comments during a strength-acknowledgment session:

"I think you are sensitive to other people's feelings. I remember when Joan was going to be left out of the roller skating party and you made sure she was invited."

"You care about poor children. Last Christmas you gave away some of your toys and stuffed animals and put that money in the Salvation Army pot."

"Boy, you run fast. I love to watch your arms and legs flying when you run in relay races at school."

"You're a great helper. It makes me feel great when we prepare dinner together."

"You're very logical and good at reasoning. You'd make a good lawyer."

"You have a great way of getting everyone to laugh. That's important for the whole family. We need to laugh."

"You have good study habits and you're very organized. That will really pay off through your whole life."

"I love to listen to your prayers. You care so much about other people and pray for them too."

"You light up my life. It's hard to put into words how special you are. You're unique and I love to see the way that you do things, the way that you react to things; you let us know it's *you* and not just the average boy-on-the-street."

"I bet you would have fun as a clown in a circus. You love to be silly. It makes people happy to be around you."

"You would be a wonderful teacher. I've seen how patient you are explaining things to your little cousins."

"It seems to be important to you to have your own money.

You want to be independent and in control. Maybe you'll start your own business someday."

"You stand up for yourself. I remember when that boy was putting down girls and you stood up to him. That was great for you and all the other girls around."

"I love to hear you sing, especially when you make up your own songs."

"You are idealistic and have a strong sense of justice."

"I'm amazed at how you can fix things. You just stick with it and tinker with it until you figure it out."

"You're a good sport and I admire that. You shake hands after the game and say, 'Nice game.' You don't tease the other team if you win."

"You're a good friend."

Instructions to the Parent-Leader

It's best to focus on just one child per session (for example, one child one evening, another child the following evening). To decide the order, let family members volunteer or pick names out of a hat. Each person usually takes about ten or fifteen minutes, depending upon the size of the family. One good plan is to have the person whose turn it is tell the family what he or she thinks his or her good points are. When that person starts running out of things to say, jump in and ask, "What do the rest of us see about _____ 's strengths and potential?" If someone is taking a turn and the rest of the family is quiet, you need to prime the pump. Once you start, the other family members will join in.

After the family seems to have covered most of the person's qualities, conclude by giving him or her the list you've written. Ask the person to read the list and share anything they learned about themselves or how they feel.

Being an Effective Leader of This Activity

Before you start the activity, give yourself a pep talk about human beings and their potential. Reaffirm your faith in their ability to grow, develop, and build from small beginnings.

Take the time to gather information about your children so that you will have enough specific ideas to share with each of them. Talk to your spouse or your child's siblings, teachers, coaches, and friends to give you specific clues about his or her qualities. Don't try this activity with your family if you can't think of several strengths to mention about each person. If you can't think of some strengths, it may help to review the list of strengths in guideline 2. Try to find and point out even emerging, fragile strengths that you can help your child build upon. It is helpful to cover a variety of areas so the child doesn't feel that he or she has only one claim to fame or only one avenue open.

Parents will inevitably value some strengths more than others. We may have our own dreams of what our child will accomplish and which talents he or she will develop. These dreams can be communicated as hopeful expectations and can have a positive impact on a child's aspirations, but we need to be aware that our goals for a child may not always mesh with the child's goals, personality, or inclinations. He or she may not want, or be able, to be the pianist or baseball player that we want him or her to be or that *we* wanted to be.

If a parent holds rigidly to a specific plan for a child's life and if the child has other interests or strengths, it will be hard for the parent to see the child's true strengths and potential and to genuinely support the child in developing it.

I believe that people who follow their interests and enjoy what they do have the best chance of excelling and contributing. The world needs each of our individual efforts. We need farmers and pharmacists, doctors and developers, engineers and entrepreneurs, mechanics and mothers, consultants and clowns, plumbers and poets. Children shine in different ways that are hard to notice if we have tunnel vision about what is worthwhile and what isn't.

Christa McAuliffe died tragically on the *Challenger* as the first teacher-astronaut. After her death, those who knew her poured out their love for her, and we learned what a special teacher she was. Yet, if we had observed her as a high school student, we might have missed this specialness. Christa was seventy-fifth out of 181 in her graduating class. She participated in sports but wasn't competitive to the point of winning at any cost. However, her homeroom teacher noticed two qualities she had: emotional stability and seriousness of purpose. Her family, friends, and students loved her genuineness, sincerity, and honesty.

In order to see the strengths and potential in a child we need to take off our blinders. If we can broaden our perspective about talents and gifts and begin to see that this child is unique, our comments will be genuine and encouraging.

RECOGNITION AND APPRECIATION

The skills and attitudes developed through the strength-acknowledgment method can be carried into daily interactions. Children thrive on having their efforts and accomplishments recognized and appreciated. "Catching" them doing something right brings positive results.

We may know this, but we don't always know how to do it. Business books constantly remind managers of the need to recognize their employees, but "lack of recognition" is close to the top of the list on survey after survey of sources of employee dissatisfaction.

Guidelines

Here are some guidelines and suggestions for recognizing achievements and showing appreciation.

1. Be specific.

It is more effective to mention the specific actions that you like than just to make general statements. The more precisely you can describe what your child did, the more aware your child will be of what you like. You also increase tremendously both your own credibility and the self-esteem of the child.

For example, saying "You're wonderful" is fine, but it doesn't explain why or how; a typical response might be, "Sure, she's my mom, she has to say I'm wonderful."

Broad, general judgments and praise are easy for children to discount. They rarely have the encouraging, esteem-building effect that parents intend. You can strengthen your comments by learning to be specific and to describe behavior. Here are some examples:

> "You've learned to borrow from the tens column when you subtract. That's great! I know it's not an easy thing to learn. Now you'll even be able to subtract big numbers."
>
> "What? You put that model together already? Let me take a look at that. That's excellent. Tell me how you did it. Those instructions look complicated but you just took your time and didn't get frustrated. You really stuck with it, didn't you?"
>
> "Grandma told me about the get-well card you sent. It meant so much to her that you thought about her and took the time to make it and send it."
>
> "I've been listening to your singing. Did you make up that song? I was just sitting here, floating away on the beautiful cloud that your music made."

Notice how the specific details create a compelling statement. Most children will feel encouraged by these comments. *Recognition maintains the achievement cycle.*

2. Be realistic.

Children don't believe unrealistic, wildly positive comments any more than adults do. Sometimes it is difficult for them to believe even the genuine ones. Work on making your encouraging statements more accurate and less extreme.

It won't always help Debbie if you say, "Oh, Debbie, you are so gorgeous! I just know that the boys won't be able to take their eyes off you. They'll all be wishing they could be your date!" If Debbie doesn't feel particularly gorgeous and if she hasn't had many requests for dates lately, these comments may be meaningless, or worse. She may say to herself, "Mom lies to me to make me feel better. She doesn't even know me and how bad I feel inside about not having dates."

It might be more effective to say, "Oh, Debbie, you look so nice. Your hair came out great and those ribbons match perfectly. I hope you have a wonderful time!"

If you avoid superlatives and absolutes like "best," "smartest," and "always," as well as predictions about amazing accomplishments, your words will have more of the desired effect.

3. Tell how the behavior helped.

When expressing appreciation of your child, follow the same guidelines for recognition, but also tell the child how his or her behavior made you feel and specifically how it helped you or the family. For example:

> "Thank you for turning the stereo off and playing quietly when I was working on the taxes. It's so complicated, but I was able to concentrate and get it done."
>
> "I appreciate that you feed the cats and change the kitty litter without my reminding you. It really helps me when you share the chores and I relax because I can count on you to do it."

"It felt great when you told me you thought I was a good mom. I guess I work pretty hard around here and it sure helps when I hear that you appreciate me."

Practice Exercises

Recognition: Select some behavior of your child, and write out a recognition message, remembering to be specific and realistic.

Appreciation: Select one of your child's actions that you appreciate. Write out an appreciation message that's specific and realistic. Tell how the action made you feel and how it helped you.

COMMUNICATING POSITIVE EXPECTATIONS

So far in this chapter we have focused on how parents can nurture children's understanding of their strengths so that children learn the kind of self-talk that will help them maintain the achievement cycle. Their beliefs about their strengths, supported by recognition and appreciation from you, will provide the impetus to positive action and positive self-talk, and thus help cultivate the achievement cycle.

Positive parental expectations—communicated in words, tone, and body language—also exert a subtle but powerful influence on a child's beliefs and actions. Emerson wrote, "Every man believes that he has a greater possibility." Parents can nurture that belief and help a child to shape and focus it.

The profound impact of expectations was demonstrated in a classic experiment using teachers and students. The study, which later became known as "Pygmalion in the Classroom," and is published under the same, was conducted by Robert Rosenthal and Lenor Jacobson.

At the beginning of the school year, several teachers were told that a series of tests had identified twenty percent of their students as "late bloomers." The students were named, and the teachers were informed that they could expect significant gains in achievement from these students for the coming year. In reality, however, there were no "late bloomer" tests; the twenty percent of the class identified as such were simply selected at random.

At the end of the year all the students were tested. The "late bloomers" had actually blossomed. Their IQ scores averaged an increase of four points, while the other students' scores remained the same.

Somehow the teachers had conveyed their high expectations to these students. Rosenthal speculated that the teachers were warmer, gave more positive feedback, responded to more questions, and challenged the students with more difficult material while transmitting to the students the belief that they could do it.

So it seems that when someone believes in you and communicates this to you in such a way that you start to believe it, that person becomes an agent for change in your life. Children, in particular, are often unaware of their talents and almost always unaware of their potential unless someone gives them clues. They don't know what they don't know.

In my seminars I ask people to think back over their lives and recall someone who took the time to point out some ability or possibility. It could have been a parent, coach, aunt, friend, guidance counselor, teacher, clergy member, or grandparent who said once or repeatedly, "You've got some ability in that area; I think you could be good at that." Here are some of the responses.

A famous public speaker from Rochester, New York, remembered that in the sixth grade a nun had told him constantly that he would be very good at talking to groups. He had never thought of it before her comments.

My friend George Van Cott was one of the smallest of sixty boys trying to make his high school football team in Brooklyn. After a couple of practices the coach said to him, "You're going to be a great quarterback." George had never thought of himself in that role, but he went on to be an All-City quarterback and starting quarterback for Boston College.

A physician told how he had been a mediocre student through high school and the first two years of college. Then one of his professors returned a paper with these comments. "Your writing style needs improvement but the ideas you presented and your reasoning indicate you have a first-rate mind." The professor's remarks made him revise his view of himself; he worked hard for the rest of his college career and was accepted into medical school.

A top real estate saleswoman on Hilton Head Island related that she was working as a receptionist when a sales manager convinced her that she had the qualities to be a good salesperson.

Baseball player Ron Oester had several mediocre seasons playing second base for the Cincinnati Reds. At the end of the 1984 season, Pete Rose became the manager and Oester improved steadily. In 1985 he was one of the top second basemen in baseball and batted .295. When he was asked what led to his sudden hitting surge, Oester described how Rose had worked with him and encouraged him. He concluded by saying, "When Pete Rose tells you that you can do something, you believe it."

Why did these experiences lead to such important changes? The person conveying the message instilled a belief, the start of an achievement cycle. Here are some guidelines that will help you communicate your positive expectations to your children so that they believe in themselves and start to act on those beliefs.

Guidelines

1. Observe and listen to the observations of others.
   In *Developing Talent in Young People* (B. Bloom, ed.), a famous concert pianist revealed in an interview that his kindergarten teacher told his parents about his enjoyment and ability in making sounds with some of the basic musical instruments. His parents followed up and supported this interest.
   Keep your eyes and your mind open for kernels of information about ability or interest.

2. Believe in your child's ability to grow and develop. See him or her in terms of what he or she can become.
   If a high school football coach looked at his crop of skinny freshmen and didn't envision them as rugged seniors, he would quit in despair. He doesn't, because he knows how they will progress.
   Don't underestimate the ability of a committed person who is pursuing something that interests him or her.

3. Base your expectations on specifics and facts as much as possible.
   Pete Rose didn't just tell Ron Oester he could be a .300 hitter. He pointed out his running speed, his bat speed, his bat handling, the chance of getting infield hits, and other qualities.

Sometimes you will need to act like a lawyer marshalling facts and building a case.

4. Be realistic about obstacles.
   Talk about obstacles, but also explain why you believe your child can overcome them. Provide support and assistance if he or she wants it: "I'm not saying it will be easy. You probably would have to give up an activity. I'm just saying that I believe if you worked at it and really want to, you could achieve it. And if it's what you want, I'll support you all the way."

5. Point out the ability, the potential, and even why you think your child should develop it, but present your ideas as suggestions, not demands.
   Dr. Mel Witmer states, "Encouragement has been described as the most powerful tool we have for facilitating growth and change while at the same time respecting the individual's freedom and right to make his or her choices."

   If you follow this guideline for communicating positive expectations, you will probably succeed in planting a seed in your child's mind. Remember that he or she wants to be more and do more, and wants your approval. Your child will probably react positively if you don't make your expectation a "should": "You have to develop your potential and you have to do it in this certain way."

   When my daughter was seven years old, I was once watching her run. I called her over and pointed out that she ran with few wasted movements and that if she *wanted* to, she could be a very fast runner. Almost before I could finish my words she said, "Daddy, do you want to see me run?" and zoomed off.

   The mother in the following example is using all of

these guidelines in talking to her daughter, who is undecided about joining the school newspaper staff.

"But Mom, I've never done anything like this. I've never been a reporter or written any stories."

"Denise, you know this will be your choice, but I want to tell you why I think you would do well on the newspaper and why I think it would be a good experience for you.

"I know that you haven't actually been a reporter or a writer before. But what do reporters do? They are interested in people. They like to talk to people and learn about them. That really describes you.

"You've also kept a diary for three years. I know that's not writing a story, but it shows that you like to write and express yourself. I think you would do a good job and enjoy it. I know this would be a challenge and you would be trying some new things. But I'm sure that the older students or the advisor or I could help you over the rough spots.

"Who knows? You might really like it and become a reporter for newspapers or TV.

"If you decide to do it, I'm behind you."

Notice the guidelines:
  Observe.
  Believe in growth.
  Give specific reasons.
  Be realistic about obstacles but communicate your belief
    that they can be overcome.
  Make it your child's choice and express your support.

Here is a simpler example:

"Heather, you're so good at math and it seems like you can design objects very accurately. Do you know much about engineers or architects? They usually are good at those two things, math and design. Would you like to learn more about them? You might be interested in those careers someday."

Practice Exercise

Design a positive expectations message to your child about a real or possible situation. Start with an easy or moderately easy message and follow the guidelines.

CHAPTER 6

ACQUIRING SKILLS BY SETTING GOALS

THERE IS OF COURSE NO SUBSTITUTE FOR WORK. I MYSELF PRACTICE CONSTANTLY AS I HAVE ALL MY LIFE. I HAVE BEEN TOLD I PLAY THE CELLO WITH THE EASE OF A BIRD FLYING. I DO NOT KNOW WHAT EFFORT A BIRD HAS PUT INTO FLYING. WHAT SEEMS EASE OF PERFORMANCE COMES FROM THE GREATEST LABOR . . . ALMOST ALWAYS, FACILITY RESULTS ONLY FROM MAXIMUM EFFORT. ART IS THE PRODUCT OF LABOR.

PABLO CASALS

Casals, the master cellist, who was still practicing and performing past his ninetieth year, presents one view of acquiring competence. Another view is demonstrated by a woman who went golfing with her friend. As they approached the golf pro he asked her, "Do you want to learn to play golf today?" She replied, "Oh no, not me! My friend wants to learn. I learned how to play yesterday."

Somewhere between learning golf in one day and practicing an instrument four hours a day for ninety-plus years there are realistic and helpful guidelines about the effort, support, and goal setting that children need to acquire skills successfully.

The attitudes, methods, and guidelines offered here apply to sports, creative arts, schoolwork, social relationships, and manual skills.

SETTING GOALS

A child who can set and accomplish a simple goal will become an adult who knows the joy of changing the world.
—Linda and Richard Eyre,
Teaching Children Responsibility

A popular insight into the need for goals is "If you don't know where you're going, any road will take you there." Goals provide a vision and a direction that motivate and shape our actions. However, achievement in most areas is a long process, and a child needs to be nourished by successfully passing milestones along the way.

When Mary Lou Retton was a young girl, she envisioned herself as an Olympic gymnast and made that her goal. This dream was important, but the dream became a reality because she also saw the specific steps that led to it. Long-range goals are helpful only if they are translated into smaller goals and action plans.

"Stretch" Goals

The most motivating goals are those that can be reached if a child stretches his or her abilities. If a goal is too easy, it is unsatisfying.

"Anybody could do that."
"That's nothing."
"I'm supposed to be able to do that."

If a goal is too hard to reach, it may appear so unlikely to be achieved that full, sincere effort isn't applied.

"It's impossible."
"No way."
"It would be a miracle."

"Stretch" goals, on the other hand, carry the message, "If I try hard and learn what I need to learn, I can do it." In order to reach the objective the child will have to grow, and be encouraged that he or she can. Therefore, "stretch" goals are *motivators* because the child believes he or she can achieve them, and gives full effort. They are also *satisfiers* because when they are reached the child feels that he or she has done something significant.

"STRETCH" GOALS: MOTIVATING AND SATISFYING

Guidelines

1. Be realistic and aim for achievability.

Take into account a child's previous performance and current abilities. In the first rush of enthusiasm and optimism, children (and adults) sometimes aim too high, too soon. This over eagerness can lead to an initial burst of activity and then to discouragement. If your child does have a lofty goal ("I'm going to run a mile a day"; "I'm going to get all As"; "I'm going to make the gymnastics team"), help him or her to set some reachable subgoals that will lead to the long-term goal.

John Naber, Olympic gold medal swimmer, recalled the long process of cutting his time from 59.5 seconds to 55.5 seconds. In each practice and meet, he set a goal of improving .01 second or more. This gradual process gave him something to shoot for, and it sustained him.

Without discouraging a child's aspirations you can say, "That's great. How are you going to build up to that?" or "How do you plan to achieve that?" or "What will you have to do to reach that goal?" Help them break it down into bite-sized chunks.

2. Build in measurability.

John Naber's subgoals were measurable. He knew when he achieved them and when he didn't. For your child to gain the maximum motivation, satisfaction, and feedback from a goal, your child needs to know whether he or she has reached it. A goal to "be a better student," "get in better shape," "be nicer to my brother," or "take better care of my pets" is too general and vague. How will you and your child know if he becomes a better student, for example? Will progress be measured by grades, homework, hours of studying, extra projects, books read, or level of enjoyment?

3. Include dates as targets.

The employee promised his supervisor, "I'll have it for you Monday." "Which Monday," asked the wary supervisor. "There are fifty-two of them every year."

Goals are more useful with dates. If your child wants to accomplish something within a realistic time period, it may be useful to include a completion date as part of the goal. Including dates in goals statements makes them stronger.

"I'm going to play that song by Christmas."
"I'm going to run a mile without stopping by May 1."
"I'll complete that science project by next weekend."

If the child doesn't accomplish the goal by the given date, he or she can use the experience to learn about time, effort, and planning.

4. Set up checkpoints.

Almost anyone's performance can be improved by placing checkpoints along the path to completing a goal. Charting progress tells us that we are on track or gives us a chance to catch up and still achieve our goal. Encourage your child to check his or her advancement towards a goal periodically, rather than waiting until a deadline and deciding "I did it" or "I didn't do it."

5. Anticipate obstacles.

Realistic goal setting involves examining potential obstacles before the final goal is set. Potential obstacles could include lack of resources ("Will I be able to get to practice?" "Do I have enough money for lessons?"), lack of skill ("Can I draw well enough to complete that project?"), or conflicts ("Can I do it even though we are going to visit my grandparents next weekend?").

If your child is setting a goal, it may help him or her to be more realistic and eventually more successful if you ask, "Is there anything that you see that could stop you from reaching that goal?" or "Are there any obstacles that might prevent you from completing that?"

6. Propose personal goals for personal control over the results.

Creating goals that involve other people or taking part in events that we don't control sometimes leads to situations where we've performed very well personally but don't achieve the goal. A child has a greater chance of success if he or she sets an achievable goal that depends mainly upon his or her own efforts and abilities.

If a child wants to set a goal like "My team is going to win the championship" or "I'm going to get the best grades in the class," guide him also to establish specific standards for his own performance. You might say, "That would be great if your team won. What do you think would make you feel like you really did a good job and helped the team" or "I'm glad you want to get good grades. You can't control what the other kids get, but what grades are you aiming for?"

7. Be flexible.

It is more the rule than the exception that children will be off target in their goal setting. They often misjudge the time required, the task's difficulty, or the number of obstacles. Rather than viewing these errors as failures, it is better to build flexibility into the original goal-setting process.

Dr. Robert Bolton, president of a management training and consulting firm in Cazenovia, New York, has designed goal-setting techniques for executives in major corporations. He advises them to set a range for their objectives from *pessimistic* to *realistic* to *optimistic*. Even without using these words you can help your child develop a range of expected results. This technique is especially useful if they are new to setting goals.

8. Provide rewards.

Children's capacities and abilities expand so rapidly that meeting goals and resetting them higher is normal and desirable. It is important, though, for a child to take the time to pause and feel good about his or her accomplishments. Too often we notice in ourselves or other adults the tendency to minimize or downplay the goal we reached and to move on swiftly to the next one.

This habit can keep us on a treadmill, a "semi-starvation diet" poor in reinforcements, sometimes without full awareness of our strengths and accomplishments. Psychologist Fritz Perls refers to it as "raising the price on yourself." To prevent your child from developing this habit, help her to pat herself on the back about her efforts and results.

CREATING SUCCESS

There are many things a parent can do to create the conditions that will help children build skills and thus reach their goals. I refer to this process as *creating success*.

Imagine a parent teaching a child to ride a two-wheel

bicycle for the first time. Knowing that the child is a beginner and that falling can be painful, the parent runs alongside to support the bike, stays close, and provides balance, until the child's effort and momentum keep the bike upright. There will be spills, but the parent's support gives the child some idea of how it feels to ride.

Novices need this kind of assistance. Most parents teach bike riding this way because it's so obvious that most children won't get the bike going on their own or will fall so often they will get discouraged or hurt.

Our children are also novices in many other areas, but their need for specific help isn't as obvious or doesn't seem as crucial. Sometimes in these situations we don't create the conditions that would increase their chances of building skills.

The Motivating Power of Small Successes

In 1981, Dr. Albert Bandura of Stanford University and Dr. Dale Schunk of the University of Houston designed an experiment that demonstrated the powerful positive impact of building on small successes. They worked with elementary schoolchildren who were doing poorly in math, didn't like math, and had little expectation of ever doing well in it. Bandura and Schunk created a teaching system that established small, achievable subgoals for the children. Instead of giving a child the overall distant goal of mastering a whole mathematical operation, they divided the task into many little steps and helped the child learn one step at a time.

The reachable subgoals provided a chance for success and the results were outstanding! The children were motivated by the immediate incentive of achieving, and their confidence and attraction to math increased as they accomplished each task. They showed persistence in solving even difficult problems and developed a positive expectation about their ability to learn math. By the end of the experiment they *sought out* math problems.

Guidelines

1. Give clear, specific instructions.
   When you're giving instructions for doing something you're very familiar with, it's common to forget what it is like to do it for the first time. You know what you want and expect, but invariably you leave something out because you assume that the person receiving the instructions will know what to do.

   Among adults, in business and at home, these assumptions lead to millions of misunderstandings and mistakes every year. If we need to improve our instructions to adults, who generally share our vocabulary and experience, think how much more carefully we need to improve our instructions for our children. Even simple chores are sometimes assigned in general terms that are open to misinterpretation:

   "Clean up your room."
   "Make your own breakfast."
   "Please cooperate."

   What are your standards for a clean room? Is any food okay for breakfast? What does "cooperate" mean? What specifically do you want them to do or not to do?

   Your best chance of producing the behavior you want is to start with specific instructions. When a child doesn't perform well at a chore or skill, ask yourself, "Did she receive instructions, and does she understand what she is expected to do?"

   I love to coach soccer, and I coached a team of six- to

eight-year-old boys and girls when my son was in that age group. One shy, slow-moving first-grader, Chuck, seemed to like kicking the ball around in practice, but in our first game he wouldn't run after the ball. After the game was over I thought about Chuck. Was he afraid of getting kicked? Didn't he want to compete?

At the next practice I talked with Chuck privately and asked why he hadn't run after the ball. His answer gave me a good laugh at myself. He told me that when I put him at fullback I pointed to a certain spot, and he thought I wanted him to stay on that spot. Chuck hadn't participated much in sports, and he had never seen a soccer game. In my haste I had assumed he knew he had to move to the ball.

With the right directions, Chuck started to love soccer. About a month later I laughed and cried when he took a ball downfield by himself, crashing through the other team in his slow, steady way, and almost scoring a goal.

In our roles as parents, teachers, or coaches we will all make the mistake I made, but we can develop the skill of giving clearer, more specific instructions. Ask yourself, "Am I leaving out any steps? Am I using words that are too general? If I didn't know anything about it, what would I need to know?"

2. Provide demonstrations.

One way to increase the chances that a child will have a clear picture of a skill or task is to demonstrate it. Even more so than adults, children need to see something before they do it. Whether you want them to learn to study for a test, add numbers, or take a foul shot, it helps to give them a blueprint. Ask yourself, "Have they seen a demonstration of how to do this correctly?"

3. Break down the task into small, achievable actions. Bandura and Schunk completely reversed children's attitudes and accomplishments by making problem solving a series of small steps. Children thrive on a diet of success; each hurdle they leap adds to their confidence and their willingness to work harder.

Success
Success   → Confidence
Success   → Motivation
Success   → Effort→ Persistence

If you can divide a task into small steps, a child starts to believe that it's possible to accomplish the task. One of the main reasons for procrastination is the fear of facing a large task. Over 200 million copies of Irving Wallace's books have been printed, yet for many years Wallace avoided completing a book.

> When I was doing short magazine pieces and screenplays, I feared undertaking anything as formidable as a book. One day, while collaborating with novelist Jerome Weidman on a screenplay for a studio, he advised me how to overcome my fear. "Think about writing one page, merely one page, every day. At the end of 365 days, at the end of a year, you have 365 pages. And you know what you have? You have a full-length book."

Small steps also serve as a guide. They give a more concrete answer to the question, "What do I do now?" Writing a book report becomes:

Finding out exactly what the teacher assigned.
Picking a book you want to read.
Reading the book.
Taking notes.
Deciding the key ideas you want to write about.

Making an outline.
Writing the first draft.
Asking someone for feedback.
Revising it.

Test taking, problem solving, and decision making can all be approached in this step-by-step way (see Chapter 9).

4. Encourage practice in a nonpressure situation.
If you think your child has a negative view of his abilities that is beginning to generate a nonachievement cycle, try to build his confidence in a situation that reduces the fear of failure.

Often children will avoid an activity or say they don't like it because they are afraid they will do poorly or lose in competition with others. While some children thrive on competition, many others have difficulties with it. There is a great deal of controversy among parents and professionals about how early and how often children should participate in competitive activities.

Dr. Tara Scanlon of the University of California, Los Angeles, researches stress and children's sports. Her findings indicate that a child's view of himself or herself as an athlete may bear little or no relation to actual ability. She found that, before a game, if a child thinks he can't do what the game demands, he almost always feels badly regardless of his actual skills.

My views are similar to Dr. Scanlon's and I offer the following suggestions for helping your child in this area.

If your child is going to compete, prepare *him or her for the activity.* The little leaguer in baseball, football, soccer, basketball, or hockey will avoid feeling like a failure if he or she has practiced and acquired some basic skills before joining a team. You may want the child to join a team in order to learn. If she has a patient coach who has enough time and who doesn't care about winning more than letting all the kids play, she might learn that way. But the chances are that she will feel like a loser if she hasn't acquired some basic skills before joining a competitive activity.

If your child is resisting an activity that you think would be fun and beneficial for her or him, find an opportunity for learning it in a nonevaluative setting. A father in Michigan learned that his daughter didn't participate in basketball games in her fourth-grade gym class. He suspected that she was afraid to do poorly, but he wanted her to get some midwinter exercise. One Sunday he invited her to play with him at the YMCA gym. As she learned how to dribble and shoot, she started to enjoy it. After two of these Sunday sessions she joined her class games.

These same guidelines apply to activities other than sports. A mother of a bright fifth-grade girl noticed that the girl had little confidence in her ability to write. She would say, "I'm not creative. I just can't think of what to say. The other kids can make up things but I can't."

The mother purchased *Writing for Kids* by Carol Lea Benjamin and worked with her daughter in an enjoyable atmosphere to do the exercises in the book. One night the girl wrote a two-page story about wild horses being captured and tamed. She loved horses and wrote the story from the horse's point of view. Her mother enjoyed the story and mentioned how original, creative, and sensitive it was to write about the horse's feelings by letting the horse tell the story.

After that the girl believed in herself as a writer. She stopped making negative comments about herself and started to spend some of her spare time writing stories.

5. Use shaping techniques.

Children are unlikely to deliver a polished performance, and we need to "shape" their efforts toward improvement. We've all seen (in ads or in person) the dolphins at Sea World jumping through a hoop ten feet in the air. The trainers didn't just wait for the dolphins to jump out of the water and through the hoop on their own. Instead, by giving them small rewards of food, they gradually trained the dolphins to jump through the water, then out of the water, and finally through a hoop. Psychologists call this process "shaping."

Your efforts to build skills in your child will be less stressful and more successful if you accept and follow the shaping process. Give children tasks they can do, on the piano or the playing field, and then look for movement in the right direction. Catch them doing it right: "that's it," "thattagirl, you're getting it," "you're really improving," "nice try," "you almost got it," "that was a lot better." These encouraging words tell the child that he or she is on the right path, and help build the bridge to competence.

6. Point out the effort that brings results.

Not everyone believes in effort. A plastic surgeon who was about to apply a local anesthetic to a man's hand in preparation for surgery when the patient asked, "Doctor, will I be able to play the piano after this surgery?" The doctor replied, "Of course you will." "That's great," said the patient, "I never could play before!"

A different philosophy about results can be seen in the story of Jim Abbott, an eighteen-year-old freshman at the University of Michigan and a phenomenal left-handed pitcher. He was offered a contract to play for the

Toronto Blue Jays, but chose college. The remarkable aspect of Jim's success is that he was born without a right hand.

In order to field and throw, Jim has taught himself a complicated but swift system of motions, transferring his glove from his stump to his left hand, then back under his right arm. He practiced throwing against a brick wall for hundreds of hours to perfect his system. Now he has a good chance to become a major league pitcher. He says, "The only thing that would have been a handicap for me is if anyone had ever been negative around me."

It is very important for children to learn that most often results are tied to effort. Study after study shows that if they attribute success only to luck or even to pure ability they will not work hard enough to develop their talents. They'll give up early or not even make the effort in the first place. The self-talk "Well, either you have it or you don't, and I don't" kills initiative.

Children will often not see the effort that goes into competence unless you point it out to them. If you don't bring it to their attention they may not realize the accomplishments that come with persistence.

The U.S. Department of Education has published a booklet, *What Works*, which Secretary of Education William J. Bennett says distills "a large body of scholarly research" on how children learn. The booklet says, "High academic achievers are not necessarily born smarter than others. Many succeed because of hard work and self-discipline. If pupils believe they have failed because they lack ability, they lose hope and stop trying."

What can you do to build children's belief in results through effort? Some suggestions follow.

Read them stories about people who achieve through

hard work. I've already shared anecdotes about Pablo Casals, Jim Abbott, and Madame Curie. You'll find others in newspapers, magazines, books, and movies.

Focus on persistence and overcoming adversity. Tell them about the Vietnamese refugee child who came to the United States unable to speak English but went on to become the national spelling champion.

Try to model persistence in your own life. Calvin Coolidge said this about persistence:

> *Nothing in the world can take the place of persistence. Talent will not. Nothing is more common than unsuccessful men with talent. Genius will not. Unrewarded genius is almost a proverb. Education will not. The world is full of educated derelicts. Persistence and determination alone are omnipotent.*

Point out that even the top performers are always learning and looking for ways to improve. Willie Mays, whom many (myself included) feel was the greatest player in baseball history, was known for the fast jump he got on balls hit to him. He seemed to anticipate where the ball would be hit. Recently he revealed that before every pitch the shortstop would put his right hand behind his back and let Willie know whether the next pitch would be a fast ball or a curve.

Teach children to attribute their own progress to effort. When children have worked to learn a skill or complete a chore, show them how their efforts have paid off. Gradually you can make them aware of what is possible through hard work and what is probable without it. As one father said to his daughter, who had set lofty goals, "Kristen, I can't guarantee you will make it if you work hard but I can guarantee you won't if you don't." (Self-discipline will be discussed in greater depth in Chapter 8.)

7. Eliminate "I can't" phrases.
   Pamela Lloyd, owner of Grenoble Stables in Granville, Ohio, is known widely for her ability to teach young adults to ride horses. Donna Boiman, president of the Central Ohio Art Academy, devotes herself to helping children develop their creative talents. Although I interviewed these women separately about their teaching strategies, they used almost exactly the same words to tell me, "I don't allow any students to say 'I can't.' "

Most occurrences of "I can't" should be challenged and replaced with phrases that focus on possibilities of improvement. If a child is saying "I can't" about a skill that he or she should learn, coach the child to say:

"I'm not yet as good at this as I want to be."
"I haven't gotten this yet."
"If I practice it I'll learn it."
"I haven't put enough time or effort into this yet."
"When I decide to work hard enough and put in the time, I'll be able to do it."

Often a child will say "I can't," but he or she can do it after being coaxed to try. These are excellent opportunities to point out that "I can't" wasn't true. Then the next time the child says "I can't," you can remind him or her that "I can't" really means "I can if I want to and if I'm willing to work at it."

Naturally it will also help if *you* avoid saying "I can't" and use a version of the useful phrases listed above. "I can't bowl" becomes "I'm not as good a bowler as I want to be but I'm working at it."

Experts on speech disorders have noted that the parents of children who eventually overcame speech problems tended to say, "He *did* not speak." Children whose parents said, "He *could* not speak" had more difficulty in improving.

CANNOT = IMPOSSIBLE = NO POSSIBILITY = SO WHY TRY?

8. Help your child to understand plateaus and slumps.
Skills are rarely acquired in a steady upward path. There are learning plateaus in all endeavors, where the students feel they are on a treadmill, stuck at one level. Sometimes it feels as if they are getting worse. This feeling can be very discouraging, especially if they are trying to do their best. For this reason it's helpful to explain to your child about plateaus, slumps, and off days.

Learning often occurs in spurts. Sometimes students practice and don't seem to be getting any better, but in fact they are preparing for the next jump in ability. Plateaus are also useful for reinforcing current skills.

When one of her riders is not improving at a particular skill and is becoming negative, instructor Pamela Lloyd suggests that they temporarily switch activities. She helps them work in an area where they can see improvement or just have fun.

The main goal is to let your child know that everyone has plateaus and slumps, and that they will end. Obviously performance can also be impaired by illness, injury, tiredness, or excessive pressure (see Chapter 7). These factors need to be checked as possible causes of performance problems.

PROVIDING EFFECTIVE CORRECTIVE FEEDBACK
Dr. Sanford Dornbush of Stanford University surveyed over 10,000 students, parents, and teachers to learn about the most effective way for a parent to confront bad grades. He

concluded: "Being visibly upset, and getting the child upset over the enormity of what he or she has supposedly done, is one of the worst possible reactions to poor grades. In fact, we've found that such a reaction leads to a decline in grades in the future." Punishment, rewards for good grades, or even no reaction were equally ineffective.

"What does work," says Dr. Dornbush, "is the low-key, positive response—offering praise for the positive aspects of a child's performance, encouraging the child to do better with those things that aren't going so well, and offering to help." If all the grades are bad, he suggests direct action through school personnel or tutors to assist the child.

In some circumstances, getting angry at children and punishing them can help them develop. In Chapter 8 we will discuss when these options are useful and necessary. Often however, performance problems can be corrected more simply and more effectively without much anger or punishment. The guidelines that follow suggest ways for providing corrective feedback.

Guidelines

1. Focus on improvement.
   Corrective feedback should contain information that can help a child improve. If you make this your goal, progress will often occur without you or your child getting too upset.

   Nine-year-old Tina was entered in two events in a local swim meet. The first event was the breast stroke, but when Tina hit the water she forgot, swam freestyle for a few seconds, and was disqualified. Between events she walked up to her father and asked, "Are you mad at me?"

   "How do you feel?" he asked.
   "I was afraid you'd be upset."

Her father smiled and said, "You'd better figure out some way to remember what event you are in."

Tina answered, "I'm going to take a second right before the start and tell myself the event."

When she was lined up for her second event, Tina seemed thoughtful. Then she looked up at her father and flashed him a big grin.

2. Be specific.

Corrective feedback is most helpful when it is specific about what the child is doing wrong and what can be done to improve. We can all improve on this approach:

"Son, how the heck could you do it that way?"
"Well, Dad, how should I have done it?"
"I don't know, but you shouldn't have done it like that!"

He gave no specific information about what his son had done wrong or what he should do differently. This advice is less than helpful if our goal is to improve performance.

Specific corrective feedback might be something like this: *"Johnny, you got a D on your last science test. That's way off what you usually get and I don't think you studied properly. One thing I noticed is that you didn't often bring home your science book. Let's figure out when you need your books before a test and how you can remind yourself to bring them home. I know if you do that there won't be any more Ds."*

3. Let your hope show through your criticism.

Parents can criticize and encourage at the same time. The message that contains information about what needs to be changed can also convey the expectation that progress will take place. For example:

"I know if you do that there won't be any more Ds."
"You're old enough to have that responsibility, and I know you will be able to handle it."

"I know what you are capable of. If you follow through on these corrections, you'll produce a fine project."

"I'm giving you this feedback because I know you can do better. You're a quick learner when you are motivated and you can understand this material."

Other Possible Reasons for Poor Performance

Poor vision, bad hearing, and learning disabilities may be responsible for problems in school or sports. These possibilities need to be investigated and corrected, if indicated, so that the underachievement cycle doesn't become firmly established.

THE NEED FOR DIVERSITY

Most of the guidelines I've presented so far are designed to keep a child working at an activity. Most activities can be fun or interesting if a child believes he or she has some ability and can improve. If you get him started, his inner desire to master things and the interesting aspects of the activity itself will help sustain his motivation. However, it is also important to expose children to different types of activities, for several reasons:

A wider variety of skills and interests will give them more choices and alternatives later in life.

They may be able to combine different skills, such as computer programming and knowledge about starting a business.

Their personal development will be more balanced.

One mother was extremely happy that her son was so motivated in school. She never had to remind him about grades because his standards were even higher than hers. She noticed, however, that he was not developing many relationships with other children. After that she began to place him in situations, like summer camp, where that part of his personality could develop.

Simply be aware that you may need to reduce the fear of evaluation or comparison that inhibits some children. The achievement cycle may have to begin gradually.

REVIEW

I have offered many guidelines in this chapter for helping your child to set "stretch goals" and for helping you to create successes for your child.

These are the key words for setting "stretch" goals:

1. Realism and achievability
2. Measurability
3. Dates
4. Checkpoints
5. Obstacles
6. Control over the results
7. Flexibility
8. Rewarding and resetting

The guidelines to help you create successes for your child are:

1. Clear, specific instructions
2. Demonstrations
3. Breaking down the task into small, achievable actions
4. Practicing in a nonpressure situation
5. Shaping
6. Results through effort
7. Eliminating "I can't"
8. Understanding plateaus and slumps

Which guidelines or suggestions are most relevant for your family? Make some notes while these ideas are fresh in your mind.

CHAPTER 7

POSITIVE SELF-MOTIVATION

NO MATTER WHO YOU ARE OR WHAT YOUR AGE MAY BE, IF
YOU WANT TO ACHIEVE PERMANENT, SUSTAINING SUC-
CESS, THE MOTIVATION THAT WILL DRIVE YOU TOWARD
THAT GOAL MUST COME FROM WITHIN. IT MUST BE PER-
SONAL, DEEP-ROOTED, AND A PART OF YOUR INNERMOST
THOUGHTS. ALL OTHER MOTIVATIONS, THE EXCITEMENT
OF A CROWD, THE STIMULATION OF A PEP TALK, THE
EXHILARATION OF A PASSING CIRCUMSTANCE, IS EXTERNAL
AND TEMPORARY. IT WOULD NOT LAST.

PAUL J. MEYER
President, Success Motivation Institute

When I grew up I often saw Timmy riding his bicycle, one
arm holding a large radio, the other waving in time to the
music. He rarely held onto the handlebars, but he rode
swiftly and skillfully for hours each day. By most standards,
Timmy was not very intelligent. His score on an IQ test
would probably have been 70 to 75. Still, Timmy loved to
ride, and he was an expert. I marveled at his balance and
speed. He almost danced as he rode.

Thinking of Timmy reminds me that human beings love
activity and strive to be competent. We have an inner drive
to develop and use our skills and to find an arena to display
them. This aspect of our nature isn't always obvious at
school or at work. Joe's supervisor at work, for example,
might describe him as unmotivated, lacking initiative, and

not caring about quality. After work, however, Joe puts on his bowling shirt and a different man surfaces: full of energy, effort, and motivation for achievement. Sometimes our goal-setting, competence-seeking qualities emerge when we have more choice and control over an activity.

ATTRACTION TO ACTIVITY

Children are drawn toward activity. It holds their interest; it's pleasurable. As they use their minds and muscles, they stretch and learn.

Activity at work, school, or play contains the possibilities of many enjoyments, rewards, and satisfactions, such as:

Joy of movement
Spontaneous action
Organizing, developing rules
Challenge, taking risks
Freedom to choose
Trying out plans and strategies
Manipulating and controlling
Stimulation and change
New information
Relaxation
Repetition and mastery
Solving problems
Teamwork and relating
Being creative
Amusement and humor
Exploring
Concentration and absorption
Joy of full effort and expending energy
Doing useful work, contributing
Encouraging and teaching others
Competing with oneself and others
Attention

Recognition and approval
Achievement

Activities—science projects, singing, or swimming—can teach many of the performance attitudes and skills that children will apply throughout their lives. Our goal is to help them enter the arena of activity and to remain there. The intrinsic rewards and their drive for activity and mastery will sustain and propel them—unless performance in the activity becomes associated with excessive pressure.

EXTERNAL MOTIVATION
External rewards for action are powerful motivators. Winning, receiving awards, or doing better than someone else are legitimate and useful reasons for exerting effort and energy toward achievement. Pressure develops when these external motivators dominate and become the major reason for engaging in an activity.

Winning: A Goal or the Goal
External motivation is useful, but when it starts to predominate, a child loses sight of all the other positive aspects of an activity: Winning is no longer merely *one* of the goals; it becomes the only goal that matters. This doesn't seem like a problem to someone who is winning, but even Superman has off days when there is too much kryptonite around.

John Wooden, the only man ever enshrined in the basketball Hall of Fame as both player and coach, made this statement:

Many people are surprised to learn that in 27 years at UCLA, I never once talked about winning. Instead I would tell my players before games, "When it's over, I want your head up. And there's only one way your head can be up. That's for you to know, not me, that you gave the best effort of which you're capable. If you do that, then the score doesn't really matter, although I have a feeling that if you do do that, the score will be to your liking." I honestly, deeply believe that in not stressing winning as such, we won more than we would have if I'd stressed outscoring opponents.

Pressure is created in a child when he tells himself how much is riding on his performance. He pushes himself into a corner where poor performance or being outdone takes on serious, even catastrophic, implications.

> "What if I blow it?"
> "If I don't do well, I'll be so ashamed."
> "She's going to be better than me."
> "I'm no good."
> "They're going to make fun of me."

Overemphasizing the achievement aspects of an activity, and especially comparing one child's performance to another's, narrows the child's focus. Self-image goes up and down with the latest measurement, subject to the vagaries of bad outings, bad luck, or someone else's good performance. The most damaging effect is the lack of attention to the intrinsic reasons for the activity.

Signs that your child may already be putting a lot of pressure on himself or herself include the following:

> Extreme nervousness before an event (test, game, performance)—shaking, stomachache, headache, crying
>
> Strong effort to avoid an activity; unwillingness to participate
>
> Loss of emotional control (crying, anger, tantrums) during an activity if losing or not performing well
>
> Bad sportsmanship
>
> Cheating or trying to subvert the performance of other children
>
> Excessive upset after loss or poor performance
>
> Extreme sensitivity to criticism

The Plimsoll Point

Every airplane has a load limit; beyond a certain weight the plane will not be able to get off the ground. This limit is called the "Plimsoll point." Every child has a Plimsoll point, too—if pressure builds beyond it, they won't be able to perform.

Dr. James Loehr has designed highly successful mental training programs for all sports. A professional athlete himself, he argues against the idea that top performers function well under pressure. In his book *Athletic Excellence: Mental Toughness Training for Sports,* he states, "One of the most significant and surprising findings that emerged from the reports of performing athletes was that mentally tough competitors do not play well under pressure . . . nobody plays well when they are feeling the pressure—not even the superstars. The difference is that skillful competitors play well in pressure situations precisely because they have eliminated the pressure."

Professional performers—musicians, athletes, salespeople, and public speakers—learn how *not* to feel excessive pressure. They use confidence, visualization, concentration, relaxation, and self-talk to achieve the best possible state. While watching athletes perform *you* may experience high blood pressure, heart palpitations, and white knuckles, but they are in a different condition.

In Chapter 10 I present some of the techniques that professionals use to reduce pressure. You can teach them to your children to help them in some of the challenging situations they face, but they will benefit even more if they learn how to reduce the pressure they feel before they enter an activity.

Guidelines for Balancing External Motivation

Each child has a different tolerance for challenge and pressure. How can a parent help a child achieve a good balance? Can we nurture the desire for good performance without crushing the many other available sources of enjoyment and satisfaction? Listed below are some guidelines for parents.

1. Emphasize other goals in addition to winning or top performance.
   After an event you can influence your child's focus by your comments or questions. If your only questions are "Did you win?" "What was your grade?" or "What did Andy get?" you are sending a message that you are interested only in results. You can balance your emphasis by adding some of these questions.

   Fun:
   "Did you have fun?"
   "Did you enjoy yourself?"
   "What did you like about it?"

   Effort:
   "Did you try hard?"
   "It's kind of fun to work hard and make that extra effort, isn't it?"

   Team play, relationships:
   "Did your group work well together on the project?"
   "Was it fun to work toward the same goal?"
   "Were you a good team member?"
   "Did you encourage the other people on your team?"

   Learning, improvement:
   "What did you learn today from this game (test, experience)?"
   "How did you improve your skills or abilities?"

   Sportsmanship, honesty:
   "Did you play a fair game?"
   "Were you a good winner or loser?"

Familiarize yourself with these questions and the list of activity rewards in the section "Attraction to Activity" earlier in this chapter. In your conversations with your child about her activities and your own, gradually expand her focus.

By emphasizing the other important aspects of involvement and action, you will provide your child with a built-in antidote to excessive performance pressure. In addition you will be elevating fun, effort, enjoyment, learning, improvement, teamwork, sportsmanship, honesty, and relationships. These values and qualities will contribute to long-term success in school, work, and family life.

2. Let your child know that there are worlds without achievement.

If you want to reduce your child's exaggerated concern with performance, guide him or her toward spending some time in nonachievement-oriented activities such as walking or hiking, observing nature, movies, talking, reading, frisbee, or fishing.

Time spent in this way will provide relaxation and balance, and will allow other qualities to emerge. If you join your child in these activities, they will provide opportunities to give attention and affection that is separate from your approval of performance. It will help him or her to feel your love and acceptance and to realize that self-worth and your love are not on the line with every test or piano recital.

3. Build a concern for others.

Dr. Benjamin Spock, whose book *Baby and Child Care* has sold 30 million copies, recently expressed this view: "Our only realistic hope as I see it is to bring up our children with a feeling that they are in this world not for their own satisfaction but primarily to serve others."

The motivation to serve and to make a meaningful contribution can be nurtured side by side with the motivation to achieve. Ted Turner is an example of this dual desire. In his roles as chairman of the Turner Broadcasting System, owner of the Atlanta Braves and Hawks, and captain of an America's Cup yacht team, his competitiveness and desire for excellence are always apparent. Yet, when he was asked about his major goals and plans for 1986, he responded, "World peace."

Turner is not an isolated example. I have had the good fortune to work with many business leaders who devote a good portion of their time, money, and skill to helping others. More and more, political and business leaders seem to be acknowledging what philosophers and spiritual leaders have long maintained about our need to find a meaningful expression of our concern for others. Dow Chemical Corporation, for example, recently launched a series of advertisements and television commercials with the theme, "Dow lets you do great things." Each one features an idealistic college graduate who wants an opportunity to make an impact on the world's problems.

This type of motivation can be introduced gradually into a child's range of values. Focusing on helping others and contributing to a family, class, or team can be emphasized along with other aspects of behavior. The questions "Did you help someone? Did you share? Did you contribute?" will become as important as "Did you win?"

Young children are concerned primarily with their own needs, and it's important to be realistic about the level of unselfishness or altruism you should expect. I think the most helpful approach is to aim for balance. A famous Hebrew saying begins, "If I am not for myself, who will be? If I am only for myself, what am I?" During the holiday season, "What will I get?" can be offset with "What will we give away?"

In addition to widening the variety of a child's motivations, you will be enhancing his self-respect and helping him find meaningful uses for his talents and resources.

SELF-MOTIVATION

Having discussed external motivation, the dangers of overemphasizing the achievement aspects of activity, and how parents can help a child balance these motivators (hence reduce the pressure they create), let us now focus on motivation that comes from within.

Dr. Benjamin Bloom's extensive research (*Developing Talent in Young People*) into the developmental patterns of concert pianists, sculptors, research mathematicians, neurologists, Olympic swimmers, and tennis champions led him to conclude that for children under ten years of age there is no known method of predicting which child will be outstanding. Long-term talent and career achievements depend heavily on the right attitudes, persistence, work habits, and openness to coaching. Many of Bloom's subjects were identified as "gifted" only after several years of hard work. Bloom suggests that parents teach attitudes and create conditions, but says that the decision for excellence comes ultimately from the child. He maintains, "If you set out to create a great talent you probably won't succeed because you'll push too hard."

Mozart's achievements in music by his sixth birthday are often noted as an example of pushing a child's talent. It is rarely mentioned, however, that his father's efforts were a *response* to his son's initial display of intense interest.

Self-Talk and Focus

Parents can teach two attitudes vital to motivation.

1. Ultimately, a child's achievements will depend on his or her degree of self-motivation—the inner desire to develop talent and potential.
2. Each individual can motivate or demotivate himself or herself by self-talk and focus.

It's important for children to be aware of examples of self-motivation because they are so accustomed to doing things when parents and teachers tell them to. You can reinforce the reliance on self-motivation in several ways.

> When someone puts forth a strong effort (running five miles, starting a business, going back to college), ask your child, "Do you think she did that because someone told her to or because she wanted to?" Point out that even if someone gave her the idea and encouraged her, she would have to motivate herself to accomplish her goal.
>
> When children make choices about pursuits and set goals, remind them that motivation is important. "Is this what you really want? I'll help you and support you, but a lot will depend on how much you want to achieve this."

Self-talk and focus are key factors in learning to manage motivation for any task or activity. Most of us just assume that we either want to do something or we don't. We don't take advantage of our ability to influence our desire by using motivating self-talk and focus.

Sometimes we actually *de*motivate ourselves by focusing on the negative parts of a task and then telling ourselves why we shouldn't do it. Here is a list of some common demotivating self-talk. How much do you feel like doing something after you express these thoughts to yourself?

> "It's boring."
> "It's too hard."
> "I hate doing this."
> "I can't do it."

"I'll never be able to do it."
"I shouldn't have to do it."
"It's not fair."
"I want to relax and have some fun. I'll get to it later."
"It's too much."
"I'll never finish it."
"I can't stand it."
"It's not that important."
"They're making me do it."
"I have to do it."
"I'll get to it someday."

If you focus on negatives and give yourself this self-talk, you make yourself want to avoid or postpone an activity even more.

Children can be taught gently to take a different approach. Explain to them, "You are only looking at all the bad things about it. That would make anyone not want to do it. Let's also look at some reasons why you might want to do it. What would be good about doing it?"

Motivating Self-Talk

When Tom Sawyer was given the job of whitewashing a huge fence, he got the other boys to do it for him by making it seem like a great thing to do. They begged him to let them do it, and they actually enjoyed themselves.

Tom was a good salesman. He talked about whitewashing in terms of the benefits and rewards. His friends became motivated, and their attitude toward the task carried through to the doing of it. Their self-talk probably was, "This is fun. I'm lucky Tom let me do this."

I don't know if Tom's specific technique will work for you the next time you want your fence painted, but you can use the principle every day. The attraction that any task holds for a person is determined by what that person tells himself or herself about it. If you want to increase your desire to do something, pay attention to the benefits, rewards, and positive aspects of doing it.

This technique of focusing on rewards and benefits is especially useful when an important task has some negative characteristics. If you decide you need to exercise regularly, for example, make a list like the following and place it where you will read it every day:

Benefits/Rewards: Regular Exercise

Develop self-discipline	Reduce blood pressure
Increase lung capacity	Control weight while
Strengthen bones and muscles	being able to eat more
Endurance, stamina	Sense of accomplishment
More energy, zest	Better mood, less
Attractiveness	depression
Stress management	Time alone (running)
Increase circulation	Break from work
strengthen heart	Fun (exercise with others)
Joy of competition	Make friends and business
Develop potential	contacts
Confidence, self-esteem	Joy of movement,
	exertion

If you make this list and read it regularly, you will be naturally drawn toward exercising.

This technique is also effective when you have long-term goals and when the payoff for hard work is well into the future (college degree, writing a book). To regularly sustain your effort, make yourself aware of the rewards.

Case Study 6, "The Book Report," in Chapter 2 contained examples of demotivation (Self-Talk #1) and positive self-motivation (Self-Talk #2). The demotivating self-talk sounded like this:

> "Why do I have to do this dumb report?"
> "It was written so long ago . . . nothing in there matters now."

"Hokey old novels—"
"I'll wait 'til next weekend."

Joshua talked himself right out of it!
The motivating self-talk sounded like this:

"I'd better make a plan . . ."
"Well, it probably won't be too bad."
"It was a classic, so the writing must be good."
"A book report isn't too hard because you can pretty much say what's in the book and how you felt about it."
". . . then next weekend I won't have it hanging over my head."

Joshua talked himself right into it!
If Joshua wanted to convince himself strongly to start the report, he could brainstorm a benefits/rewards list:

Benefits/Rewards: Completing Book Report This Weekend

"I'll read a classic book with good writing."
"I'll have more time to do the report and get a better grade than if I wait until the last minute."
"I'll need to learn to do reports well because I'll have a lot of them in college."
"I'll be increasing my self-discipline."
"If I don't do it, I'll be worrying about it all week."
"It's enjoyable to write down ideas."
"I'll feel good about myself, and have a sense of accomplishment."
"I'm going to reward myself when I'm done by renting a movie, buying some ice cream, and inviting a friend over."

If your child is too young to write down a list, you can teach these mental habits verbally or have him dictate his list while you write it.

Here's another example. When winter is over and you decide to clean out the garage for spring, your child might balk at helping out. You could approach it this way: "I guess there will be some hard things about cleaning out the garage, but let's get ourselves in the mood by figuring out all the good reasons for doing it."

> "We can put all the winter things down in the basement and have more room."
> "It will be easier to reach the toys, tools, and furniture we use during the spring."
> "It's a lot safer when there is less clutter."
> "We'll be able to open the car doors without scratching them or knocking over your bike."
> "The garage will look nice when it's clean."
> "We'll feel like we accomplished something and did our share to help the family today."
> "After we finish we can take our bikes out for a ride and I'll buy you a soda."

In addition to this technique, which a child can learn to use for chores, schoolwork, tests, or practices, the following self-talks are useful:

> "I motivate myself by what I think about."
> "When I want to have a stronger desire to do something I can think of the rewards for doing it."
> "There are things I like and things I don't like about some activities. If I accept the things I don't like and pay more attention to the things I like, I'll feel more like doing them."
> "If I have to do something, I won't make it any easier by going over and over what's bad about it and why I don't want to do it."
> "My parents, teachers, and coaches can encourage me, and it really helps. But in the end I'm responsible for motivating myself if I want to reach my goals."

REVIEW

In this chapter I presented the following key ideas:

Intrinsic versus external motivation
The self-talk and signals of excessive pressure
Guidelines for balanced motivation
   Emphasizing other goals (fun, effort, team play, relation-
      ships, learning, improvement, good sportsmanship)
   World without achievement
Building a concern for others
Responsibility for self-motivation
The self-talk of self-motivation
Motivating and demotivating self-talk
Benefits/rewards list
Useful self-talk

Can you see signals of excessive pressure or demotivation in any of your family members? Note who they are and specific examples of their negative attitude.

Now list how you plan to encourage positive self-motivation in each individual.

CHAPTER 8

BUILDING RESPONSIBILITY AND SELF-DISCIPLINE

WE CANNOT SOLVE LIFE'S PROBLEMS EXCEPT BY SOLVING THEM. THIS STATEMENT MAY SEEM IDIOTICALLY TAUTO- LOGICAL OR SELF-EVIDENT, YET IT IS SEEMINGLY BEYOND THE COMPREHENSION OF MUCH OF THE HUMAN RACE. THIS IS BECAUSE WE MUST ACCEPT RESPONSIBILITY FOR A PROBLEM BEFORE WE CAN SOLVE IT. WE CANNOT SOLVE A PROBLEM BY SAYING "IT'S NOT MY PROBLEM." WE CANNOT SOLVE A PROBLEM BY HOPING THAT SOMEONE ELSE WILL SOLVE IT FOR US. I CAN SOLVE A PROBLEM ONLY WHEN I SAY "THIS IS MY PROBLEM AND IT'S UP TO ME TO SOLVE IT."

M. SCOTT PECK
The Road Less Travelled

NOW OR LATER?

Dr. Peck's book has been immensely popular even though the first heading is "Problems and Pain," the first sentence is "Life is difficult," and the title of the first chapter is "Discipline." The foundation of his approach is discipline, which he defines as "the basic set of tools we require to solve life's problems."

In one sense Peck's appeal is similar to the warning of the mechanic in the oil filter commercials who points to a useless engine and says, "You can pay me now, or you can pay me later." Children can learn responsibility, delayed gratification, and self-discipline from us now or more painfully from society later.

Some parents want to spare their children pain and hardship. One day a huge stretch limousine eased into a parking space on Park Avenue in New York City. A chauffeur emerged, quickly opened the door for a luxuriously tailored woman, and then carried out her ten-year-old son on a velvet cushion.

A passerby noticed the boy and asked his mother, "Can't the boy walk?" She replied icily, "Of course he can. But fortunately he doesn't have to."

LIFTING A COW

A tourist was visiting the ranches of Argentina when she saw a teenaged boy walk over to a cow and lift it off the ground. She was fascinated, and asked him why he did it and how he got to be that strong. The boy explained, "Two years ago my father gave me a baby calf. He told me to come out here every morning and every evening and lift it off the ground. I have done that. As the calf grew, I also became bigger and stronger. The cow you saw me lift is that same one. My father let me keep it."

The boy's father devised an excellent plan to develop his son's strength and his concern for an animal. Children acquire responsibility and self-discipline gradually. It is an ongoing process, shaped continually by everyday choices and the consequences of those choices. Responsibility can't be transferred to children through lectures delivered from time to time. It is built upon and tested by small interactions each day.

If we want to make *responsibility* and *self-discipline* important objectives for our children, we must evolve effective plans and strategies.

STRENGTHENING A CHILD'S "WILL DO"

In previous chapters I offered guidelines and suggestions for expanding your child's "can do"—your child's abilities. I recommended the attitude of a learner, clear instructions, demonstrations, simplified tasks, shaping, and other methods for increasing the likelihood that a child will be able to perform successfully.

Still, not all problems are related to "can do" issues. Sometimes the deficit is in the area of effort, determination, commitment, or persistence. It is a "will do" problem: a matter of motivation, not ability.

Often problems develop in both areas because children rapidly lose their "will do" for tasks they think they can't do. It will be useful, however, to concentrate on motivation as a separate area of concern and discover what a parent can do to strengthen a child's "will do" qualities.

The Link to Self-Esteem

In his pioneering study *The Antecedents of Self-Esteem*, the psychologist Stanley Coopersmith found that children with higher levels of self-esteem came from families that, among other things, demonstrated more love and acceptance than criticism; emphasized fairness and mutual respect; and *were not permissive* in that there were clearly stated and consistently enforced rules.

In *The Stress-Proof Child*, authors Antoinette Saunders, Ph.D., and Bonnie Remsberg, Ph.D., state, "Children are constantly looking for limits. They look for consistency because it means that whomever they depend on is putting energy and effort and love into caring for them."

Dr. Thomas Connellan investigated the remarkable achievement characteristics of first-born children (twenty-one of the first twenty-three astronauts, for example, were first-born even though statistically only one-third of all children are first-born). He found that these children were consistently given more responsibility than other children in the family. He also learned that parents gave the first-born more feedback and conveyed higher expectations. His findings are presented in *How to Grow People Into Self-Starters*, an excellent book for parents and managers.

This research on self-esteem and achievement verifies accepted wisdom. Sophocles told us, "If men live decently, it is because discipline saves their very lives." The Bible advises, "He who loves his child is diligent to discipline him."

Let's spell out specifically how developing responsibility and self-discipline raises a child's self-esteem.

DEVELOPING SELF-CONTROL

When I worked as a psychologist in mental hospitals I learned that one of the most terrifying experiences a person can suffer is to lose control of his or her thoughts and actions. Exercising some degree of control is basic to our identity and self-confidence.

Children learn gradually to control themselves. As they gain the ability to act or not to act, their inner power increases. They feel more confident that they can respond to the demands and limits of their world; a child without inner control is frightened, and correctly so. Through anticipation and control children gather rewards and avoid negative consequences. Their environment will demand that they learn to delay gratification; achieving self-control is the first step.

COPING

Dr. Albert Bandura of Standford University found that self-efficacy was related not only to confidence in current skills but also to faith in one's ability to respond to unexpected difficulties.

LEARNING PERSISTENCE

Self-discipline enables a child to stay on the path to his or her goals and see things through from beginning to end. This leads to success and feeds the achievement cycle of positive self-talk, sustained effort, and desired results. Ray Kroc, the late founder of the McDonald's Corporation, stated, "The essential factor that lifts one man above his fellows in terms of achievement and success is his greater capacity for self-discipline."

CONTRIBUTING

One of the greatest foundations for a sense of self-worth is the belief that one is making an important contribution to the family or community. Children who take on these responsibilities and fulfill them expand their positive self-image.

TAKING RESPONSIBILITY

Related to the feeling of contributing is a child's belief that he is doing his share, that he is a responsible member of his family. Responsibilities are often assigned early in life. If a child's "I'm responsible" self-talk becomes established, the child becomes an adult who asks himself, "What are my responsibilities in this situation?" and struggles with the question, "What would be the responsible thing to do?"

We can be responsible *to* families, schools, and communities, but we are also responsible *for* ourselves. The major concern of Scott Peck's book is accepting personal responsibility for our problems and the results of our actions. If a child learns to take responsibility for her decisions or indecisions, actions or inactions, she greatly increases the chances for improving those choices and behaviors.

People who are willing to look at their contribution to a problem are less likely to repeat the problem. They therefore set themselves on the achievement cycle to self-esteem.

RESISTING PEER PRESSURE

At some point intense peer pressure will be exerted on your child. He or she may be urged to act irresponsibly concerning alcohol, illegal drugs, vandalism or theft, cheating in school, sexual conduct, reckless driving, or cruelty to others.

Resisting peer pressure requires inner discipline. The inability to resist weakens a child's self-regard because he does things he is ashamed of, and he knows he wasn't strong enough to say "no" to the group's demands.

Guidelines and Suggestions: The Discipline Dozen

The following principles will guide you in teaching children responsibility and in developing their inner strength. Particularly for these goals, how you model these attributes and how you react to their behaviors is more potent than what you say. Using these techniques and approaches will create the habits and self-talk of responsibility.

1. Assign clear, nonoverlapping responsibilities.
2. Emphasize their choice, their responsibility.
3. Inspect what you expect.
4. Be firm and consistent.
5. Conduct progress reviews and encourage self-evaluation.
6. Respond to cheating.
7. Encourage meaningful contributions.
8. Teach the value of work.
9. Encourage responsibility to society.
10. Strengthen will power.
11. Overcome frustration.
12. Anticipate peer pressure.

Let's examine each of these guidelines.

1. Assign clear, nonoverlapping responsibilities.

Confronting behavior problems and irresponsibility is an important parental role. Why not explain rules and assign responsibilities in a way that gives children the best chance to behave correctly?

Clarity. In Chapter 6, I discussed the benefits of clear, specific instructions in furthering the acquisition of skills. This clarity is equally important when assigning responsibilities.

These two objectives should guide your actions:

> "I want to explain and/or demonstrate exactly what I expect my child to do, and by what time, and to answer any question he has. My goal is to create the conditions for my child to meet the expectations successfully."

> "I want the responsibilities to be clear so that if he does not fulfill them it will be easy for him to see that it was because of his actions or inactions."

These are the key, ever-present goals. You want your children to meet their responsibilities; if they don't, it is important that they see themselves as accountable. The urge to make excuses for poor performance is very strong. I don't know any way to eliminate it completely, but specific instructions reduce such excuses:

> "I didn't know you wanted me to do that."
> "You never told me I was supposed to do it that way."
> "You didn't tell me I shouldn't do that."

Let them know what you are going to hold them accountable for.

> "Right after supper each night I'm expecting you to clear the dishes and silverware off the table, put the scraps under the sink, wash and dry the dishes, and then put them away. This is what I consider a clean dish and this is how dry it should be before you put it away."

This explanation is more helpful than "After we eat supper I want you to clean up," which is vague about exactly what you want done or what you would consider an acceptable job.

Nonoverlapping responsibilities. When more than one person is assigned a task, the possibilities of passing the buck or blaming someone else are substantially increased. Even "I want *you* to clean up" is better than "Kids, after we eat, I want you *both* to clean up." When a parent tries to separate chores, an excuse like this may surface:

> Parent: "Johnny, you are supposed to keep your own room clean. Now it's messy, so let's get going."
> Johnny: "Allison messed it up too. She should help me."

All Allison did was leave a gum wrapper in his room two hours before, but Johnny is trying to put her on the hook with him.

You can reduce this avoidance pattern and move your children toward being accountable by taking a little extra time to define and divide areas of responsibility wherever you can. Then it is clear who did or didn't do what they were supposed to do.

2. Emphasize their choice, their responsibility.
   Children can learn a variety of ideas about being responsible for one's choices and actions: They can learn that parents are their personal servants. They can learn that no one will hold them accountable for their choices. If they learn these lessons they are probably headed for trouble. Their friends and teachers are unlikely to relish catering to them, and society in general certainly will expect them to take the consequences of their decisions.

   We want our children to increase their capacity for

shouldering responsibilities, so we assign certain chores or ask them to start doing some things for themselves. Eventually they will make choices and decisions of their own, which carry duties.

> "I want a dog."
> "I want to take guitar lessons."
> "I need money. I'm going to deliver newspapers."
> "If I get a new bike I'll take good care of it."

A parent often wants to encourage a child to take on some of these responsibilities, and can go a step further to strengthen the connection between choice and accountability.

To reinforce the fact that a child is making a choice, a parent can use these phrases where appropriate:

> "If you want to . . ."
> "You decide about that . . ."
> "It's really up to you . . ."

Then help them explore the probable duties that will result from the decision:

> "You would have to get up earlier to take the dog for a walk."
> "Your guitar teacher would expect you to practice during the week."

You can provide support:

> "We can get you an alarm clock if you want to get up earlier."
> "We can work out a practice schedule and a way to remind you if you are not willing to practice as much as the teacher suggests."

In any case, always emphasize their choosing or deciding and the specific responsibilities that result from these choices.

3. Inspect what you expect.

It's vital to follow through on the rules and responsibilities that have been established. When you check to see that rules are observed and chores completed satisfactorily, you send the message that you meant what you said.

Children will thus learn that they won't be able to evade responsibilities or bypass agreements. Although they may balk or complain, they will adjust to your limits and expectations. Their "will do" character grows as they sense your commitment to following through.

4. Be firm and consistent.

Firmness is an all-purpose skill. It helps you take the middle path in retaining control of yourself and the situation.

Giving in		*Getting more* *angry than necessary*
—————————	*Firmness*	—————————
Losing control of *the situation*		*Losing control of* *yourself*

Most parents will bend the rules and make exceptions once in a while, but if they cave in regularly about rules and chores, children don't know when they will "get away with it" and when they will "get it."

Salespeople like to say, "In every situation a sale is made. Either you sell the customer on why he should buy or he sells you on why he shouldn't." Children often demonstrate great sales skills. They aren't afraid to "ask for the order," and can wear you down with persistence. At these times, it is important to remain firm in your goal of gradually strengthening their inner discipline.

Firmness will also help you achieve behavior standards

with your child without excessive anger, spanking, or
name-calling, which you may regret later. Here is some
self-talk that will help you act firmly and consistently.

> "These rules are fair. These chores are reasonable. My
> child needs to learn to obey rules, develop inner disci-
> pline, and become responsible. It is my responsibility as
> a parent to train him in this way."
>
> "The loving, caring thing for me to do is to be firm and
> insure that he does what he is supposed to do. It may
> seem hard for both of us now but when he senses my
> firmness and resolve it will get easier."
>
> "Once she knows that the rules will be enforced and I
> follow up on the chores, she will stop resisting so much."

5. Conduct progress reviews and encourage self-evaluation.
   If you make a regular progress check of responsibilities
   and projects, you give a child a better chance for correction along the way. When the pet has died from malnu-
   trition, the project is overdue, or the D is on the report
   card, there is not much to do except be upset and try to
   learn from it, but if parents monitor performance periodically, they can detect potential problems and help
   the child avoid them.

   Assessing progress at shorter intervals also strengthens
   the connection between children's actions and the results
   of those actions. They can see more clearly what they
   have done or not done. A powerful way to review progress
   and introduce self-evaluation is to conduct short accountability sessions every week. You might ask, "Looking over your chores and responsibilities at home
   (school, church), how do you think you've done this
   week?" Then you can discuss your child's views and
   share your opinion. You'll be learning a lot and conveying to your child how important being responsible is to
   you.

Self-evaluation helps reinforce commitment and accountability. By using this method regularly you will teach your child the skills of self-assessment and correction that he can use the rest of his life.

6. **Respond to cheating.**
Pressure to perform and intense competition promote cheating in school and sports. Michael Stone, a writer for *New York* magazine, researched the academic pressure in New York City's top high schools and reported claims that cheating has reached epidemic proportions. He states, "Particularly disturbing is the fact that those who cheat include not only the lazy and the disaffected but also the brightest and most conscientious students."

When children cheat they weigh the payoffs—for example, better grades or winning a game—against the risks of getting caught, but they rarely have the perspective to understand the internal rewards or risks unless these are explained. It is important to talk with children about how cheating erodes integrity and can make them feel bad about themselves. People often forget grades and victories, but can remember even childhood instances when they cheated. Someone who cheats may always wonder, "Would I have won that game if I hadn't cheated?"

In addition, children need to know that integrity earns rewards in self-esteem and relationships as well as in the marketplace. A Forum Corporation study established that top salespeople were more productive because their customers trusted them, not because they were more persuasive.

7. **Encourage meaningful contributions.**
Even two-year-olds can help the family: putting things away, cleaning up, handing things to Mommy, sorting

laundry. As children grow up they can assist in sweeping, washing dishes, shopping, cooking, and yard work. Even if their helping out occasionally slows you up or causes more work, it is an important part of their development. It teaches the following:

> Families help each other. They divide work and responsibilities.
> Mom and Dad take care of me as I grow up but they are not my personal servants. I must learn to do some things for myself and even do some things for them.
> I'm doing my share. The family needs me. I feel big when I help.

Dr. John Obedzmski of the Center for Families and Children has found that five-year-olds who perform small household chores report feeling important and say that they are contributing to the family.

Let children know how their efforts help you: "It's such a relief to be able to count on you to mow the lawn every week. It looks great."

8. Teach the value of work.

Harvard Medical School, under the direction of Dr. George Vaillant, conducted a forty-year study of the lives of 456 teenage boys from inner-city Boston. The primary finding was that boys who worked, even at simple household chores, enjoyed happier and more productive lives than those who did not. Dr. Vaillant declares, "It's not difficult to explain. Boys who worked in the home or community gained competence and came to feel they were worthwhile members of society. And because they felt good about themselves, others felt good about them."

Linda and Richard Eyre, authors of *Teaching Children Responsibility*, claim,

"All work and no play" make Jack a dull boy, but it doesn't happen very often today. The more frequent occurrence is "all play and no work"—and that makes Jack an unresponsible boy!

They emphasize (and I agree) that children learn important lessons about work and money when they start to earn money of their own. With their own children they follow this pattern:

During ages eight to twelve while the children do earn their own money and buy their own things, it is usually us that they earn it from. When they turn twelve, however, they are expected to earn it elsewhere—from paper routes, baby-sitting and other out-of-the-home sources.

I recommend that parents assign some chores that children do simply because they are part of a family, and then offer extra jobs that allow them to earn money.

9. Encourage the responsibility to society.
From 1982 to 1986, Bob Wieland walked across America—on his hands. Bob lost his legs in Vietnam after a 1969 mortar blast, but using hand pads and a strong upper body he took five million "steps" in his "Spirit of America Walk for Hunger." As he traveled from California to Washington, D.C., Bob spoke to many children's groups. In one community he said:

The Bible says, "We that are strong ought to bear the infirmities of the weak and not to please ourselves." That's really close to my heart. Basically I try to stress the importance of setting goals, overcoming obstacles, and commitment in everyday life. We've all been given a talent. God has a beautiful plan for you if you get your priorities straight.

Children can be introduced gradually to the idea of responsibility to society. Here are some suggestions:

Discuss how different occupations (nurse, teacher, truck driver, parent, homemaker) fill needs in the community in addition to providing support for the individual and his or her family.

Have occasional conversations about local, national, or world problems and what people are doing to solve them.

Explain that each of us has a concern for ourselves and for others. We can learn and grow because it's exciting to develop our potential, and we have a special feeling when we use some of our time, energy, and talent to help others.

10. Strengthen will power.

Inner strength is like muscular strength: use it or lose it. Muscles grow stronger when they are required to work. To develop children's "will do" capacity, we must sometimes provide situations where they need to make a sustained effort to get what they want. We need to be different from Charlie's family.

Charlie was an eight-year-old boy who had never spoken. Then one morning at breakfast he said, "The oatmeal is cold." His parents were shocked. These were the first words he had ever spoken. They asked, "Charlie, why didn't you ever speak before?" Charlie replied, "Up to now everything has been fine."

Children need to develop and learn about their inner reserves. When a child knows that he or she can dig deeper and respond to tough situations, that child has a special confidence and a positive self-image.

Our goal is to help a child gradually use and believe this self-talk:

"I have inner strength."
"There are inner reserves I can call on."
"Sometimes I can do more than I think I can."

"Sometimes it feels good to try as hard as I can."
"It feels good to stick with something and complete it."

To build inner strength, you can set up activities that "stretch" the amount of work or effort a child thinks he or she is capable of. I'm certainly not advocating Marine boot camp, but there is a range between what a child thinks he can do and what you suspect he can do. Possible activities include:

Yard work
Cleaning out the garage
Long walks, hiking
Bike rides
Camping (requires gathering wood and "roughing it")

After these activities emphasize these points:

"You felt like quitting but you didn't. Doesn't it feel good to stick with it and finish?"
"You got a 'second wind,' didn't you? Everyone has a reserve of strength inside they can draw on when they need it."
"You did a lot more than you thought you could. Many times you will be amazed at what you can do when you make up your mind and make the effort."

11. Overcome frustration.
Frustration occurs when we don't get what we want when we want it. Learning to deal with inner frustration is a key to being able to control impulses, delay gratification, and work toward longer-term goals. Here are some suggestions to help your child improve in this area.

Acknowledge frustration in your child and point it out. "It's frustrating not to be able to tie your shoe yet, isn't it? You'd like to do that now and you're frustrated, aren't you?"

Point out that everybody feels frustrated sometimes.

"Frustration is something everybody feels. We don't always get what we want when we want it. Sometimes it takes a long time and a lot of work to learn how to do things or earn enough money to buy things we want. It can be frustrating when other people don't do what we want them to do, and we can't control them."

Emphasize improvement. Every child will eventually handle frustration in some way even if it takes a while. When they do, reinforce it with comments like these:

"That was frustrating, but you handled it."
"Doesn't it feel good to get over feeling frustrated? You feel a little stronger inside, a little more in control."
"You might not always handle frustration this well, but this shows you that you can."

12. Anticipate peer pressure.

Children are often faced with peer pressures as well as inner impulses. True inner discipline comes from learning to respond correctly to both types of pressure. Even a self-disciplined child is vulnerable to group pressure if he or she doesn't have the skill to resist the demands and arguments of people they think of as friends.

In addition to giving children needed information about the risks of smoking, drugs, alcohol, drinking and driving, sexual behavior, and other hazards, go one step further and help them acquire the self-talk and words to defend themselves.

With your child, anticipate the pressures he or she will experience and rehearse self-talk and actual dialogue. Ellen Rosenberg, author of *Getting Closer: Discover and Understand Your Child's Secret Feelings About Growing Up*, states,

Facts alone aren't enough. They must be used correctly when it is time to make a decision. That means teaching

your child to stick to his guns in the face of ridicule. It's very hard for a child to say no to friends who are pressuring him. He'll feel much more comfortable if you offer specific phrases or responses that he can use when he is saying no to a friend.

Here is some helpful self-talk to review with your child:

"It's very likely that I will experience pressure from someone to do things that are not good for me or go against my values."

"I'll have a choice; to be true to myself or give in to get that person's approval."

"Kids try to get you to do things because they already feel guilty and know they are wrong. If they can get you to do what they are doing it makes them feel better."

"Friends who try to get you to do something that is no good for you and won't take no for an answer are not real friends."

"A true friend will respect my choice."

"If I follow my own beliefs and values I may have to stand alone sometimes. It's worth it. I can make other friends and I'll like myself better."

"Kids may tease me that I'm chicken or a sissy or always do what my parents say. If I want to take risks or disagree with my parents I'll do it when I want to, not when other kids tell me to."

"I can say NO. I'm proud of that."

"It's wrong to hurt other people or their property. No one is going to talk me into doing that."

"I'll state my opinion and then walk away if I feel they don't really want to hear my opinion and respect my decision."

These are only a few ideas. You can greatly improve your child's ability to resist pressure by discussing this self-talk and letting her work out her own plan of self-talk and responses.

CHAPTER 9

PROBLEM-SOLVING AND TEST-TAKING SKILLS

WE BELIEVE THE BEHAVIOR OF HAPPY CHILDREN IS A
RESULT OF UNCONDITIONAL LOVE AND STRAIGHT, CONSIS-
TENT, CARING PARENTAL INSTRUCTIONS, AND DEMON-
STRATIONS OF HOW TO THINK AND SOLVE PROBLEMS.
AMY BJORK HARRIS AND THOMAS HARRIS
Staying OK

If the only tool you have is a hammer, pretty soon the
whole world starts to look like a nail. Children need a
variety of "tools," including problem-solving skills and
strategies, to meet the range of challenges and opportunities
that face them. Thus, in addition to a basic body of
knowledge, children need abilities in thinking, decision
making, and problem solving. Part of the foundation of a
child's self-image is the child's view of his or her ability to
solve everyday problems. The goal is to help a child acquire
this self-talk:

> "I can solve problems."
> "My mind helps me solve problems."
> "I'm resourceful. I can think of strategies and plans to solve
> problems."
> "Solving problems can be fun. You get to use what you
> know and test out ideas."
> "Knowing I can solve problems gives me confidence about
> the future."

"I love challenges."
"I like taking tests."

This chapter discusses some methods that will help your child become a better problem solver *and* a better test taker—since test-taking skills are similar to problem-solving skills.

SELF-INSTRUCTION PROBLEM-SOLVING MODELS

Language can be used to guide and regulate behavior. Dr. Donald Meichenbaum, author of *Cognitive Behavior Modification*, and other cognitive psychologists have developed programs that rely on verbal self-instructions to guide a child towards more effective problem solving.

Initially an adult serves as the model and instructs himself out loud as he works on a problem. Then the child is encouraged to solve a problem, repeating the instructions and being coached by the adult when necessary. The goal is to help the child achieve cognitive control by channeling behavior through thoughts and verbal instructions.

The problem-solving model consists of these steps:

Problem definition
Problem approach or strategy
Focusing attention
Error detection and correction
Coping statements
Self-reinforcement

In practice it may sound like this:

Problem definition:
"Okay, what do I have to do?" (Describe task.)

Problem approach or strategy:
"I have to go slowly and carefully."
"I'll check my work on each problem."

"I'll look at all the choices before I pick one."
"I'd better make sure I have all the pieces, tools, and instructions."

Focusing attention:
"Stop, look, and think before I answer."
"I'm not going to look around. I'm going to keep doing my work."
"I need to ask myself what this story means."
"These tasks are easy if I just take my time."
"I'd better watch what I'm doing."

Error correction:
"Oh, I did it wrong."
"I need to circle the words I don't understand."
"I'll have to ask for help."
"If I had listened more carefully I would have understood the assignment."
"Oops, I made a mistake. Good thing I checked."

Coping statements:
"It's only a mistake. Now I'd better correct it and be more careful."
"Even if I made a mistake I can fix it and go on."
"I'll do the best I know how right now and then find out how to improve."

Self-Reinforcement:
"I did it!"
"I'm getting it!"
"It's working."
"I can handle this."
"Great! I followed my plan and it worked."
"I solved it."

This approach is very useful with elementary school children, and I also recommend it strongly with preschool and kindergarten-level youngsters.

In 1976, researchers B. Camp, G. Blom, F. Herbert, and W. Van Doorwick designed "Think Aloud," a simpler version of this problem solving model. With the help of cards a child learns to ask, "What is my problem? What is my plan? Am I using the plan? How did I do?"

Pick school tasks, puzzles, or something that needs to be fixed or assembled, and model this problem-solving approach using the actual words. You can invite your child to do a similar problem using self-instructions or you can rely on your child's observing you to learn an effective approach and a positive attitude toward problems. Early positive experience with problem solving will shape children's attitudes about themselves and increase their curiosity and persistence.

GENERAL PROBLEM-SOLVING SEQUENCE

As children grow older you can model and actually explain a general sequence of steps for finding good solutions to a variety of problems.

1. Define the current problem completely.
   What are the specific characteristics of this problem? It is often said that if you can define a problem accurately you are more than halfway toward resolving it.

2. Gather useful information.
   What do I know that would be useful? What do I need to know to solve the problem?

3. Brainstorm a list of solutions, alternatives, or strategies for dealing with the problem.
   Brainstorming is a form of creative thinking, and it allows a person to entertain a wide variety of alternatives before choosing. During brainstorming, let ideas emerge uncensored and without evaluation. At the next stage, ideas are evaluated and then discarded, used, or modified. Let

your children practice brainstorming some of these questions:

> How could we save money?
> What are fun things to do that don't cost money?
> How can we help the community?
> How could we cut our electric bill?
> What are different ways we could exercise our bodies?
> What are the ways a person could make new friends?

4. **Evaluate the consequences of each alternative.**
This is an important step for children to learn. When they get in trouble, it is often because they didn't think through the consequences of their actions. Each choice has pros and cons, and they need to be considered before a decision is made.

In her book, *Getting Closer,* Ellen Rosenberg gives an example of a teenager considering the possible consequences of resisting peer pressure to drink beer at a party:

> "Friends may accept my decision."
> "Friends may continue to pressure me."
> "Friends may tease me and reject me."
> "I may feel proud that I'm strong enough not to give in."
> "I won't get into trouble."
> "Driving home will be safer."

There are other choices (having a beer, leaving the party, trying to get the other kids to stop drinking) with various consequences. Thinking about the range of alternatives and possible outcomes yields informed decisions.

5. **Decide and implement.**
Results aren't guaranteed, no matter how well we think through alternatives. At some point we need to choose and then implement a course of action.

6. Monitor performance and observe outcomes.

A plan may solve a problem, provide only a partial solution, or give information only about what doesn't work. If it works, pat yourself on the back and study what you did right so you can do it again when needed.

If the problem still remains, go through the problem-solving process again using the information gained from implementing the first alternative.

Your problem-solving style will invariably influence your child's style. No matter how you may have reacted to problems in the past, you will have many opportunities to improve and demonstrate a new system. Fortunately or unfortunately, life will probably continue to furnish personal, family, and work problems. Your willingness to face these problems and work systematically toward solutions will strongly influence your child's attitude in this area.

TEST-TAKING SKILLS AND STRATEGIES

The United States is a test-taking country. We use tests to measure basic skills, to measure the ability to learn, and for placement in classes, teams, and jobs. We may not like the excessive reliance on testing and we may question whether tests really measure what they say they measure, but our children are likely to be tested regularly.

We can think of test-taking skill as a particular problem-solving skill. In this case the "problem" is the test. Just as general problem-solving skills give us a method for approaching a problem, so test-taking skills give us a method for approaching a test. Although we think we may know the answers, the way in which we proceed to deal with test questions will help us reduce the pressure of the test-taking situation and thus help us be more successful in taking the test.

The ability to take tests well is helpful, and without this ability a child can be severely handicapped. Poor performance can lead to text anxiety. This fear of failure becomes a self-fulfilling prophecy as nervousness and self-doubt erode a child's actual abilities.

The positives in this situation are that children, even first graders, can learn simple test-taking skills and strategies.

A mother in one of my seminars talked to Amy, her second-grader, before Amy took ability and achievement tests. She suggested that if Amy got stuck on a problem she should skip it, do the ones she knew, and then come back to it if she had time. When Amy came home after the tests she gave her mom a huge hug and shouted, "Mommy, I did it. I did what you said, and when I did the problem again I got the right answer."

When the mother told me about it, she was more excited than Amy. Parents want to be effective, and they need the reinforcement of seeing their efforts lead to positive changes in their children.

Here are some test-taking guidelines.

1. Don't cram.

Learning comes from studying that takes place over a period of time. Cramming rarely leads to retained information, and it can add easily to stress and test anxiety.

2. Learn strategies for using time.

Children can get stuck on one question or problem and lose valuable time necessary for answering the rest of the test. Make them aware of this tendency and help them plan a strategy of skipping difficult questions and moving on to the questions they can answer. When they return to the difficult ones, they are usually more confident, find the questions to be clearer, and are thus more successful.

3. Pay careful attention to directions.

   Many children make mistakes simply because they don't read carefully and follow directions. Include this step in their self-instructions. "Read the directions carefully. If I don't understand I'll ask the teacher to explain."

4. Check answers carefully.

   Children make simple mistakes that can be corrected if they recheck their answers. Encourage them to do this when they have time, especially if there is a series of problems in which one answer depends on previous work.

5. Guess, when appropriate.

   Children need to know that guessing is an appropriate strategy in certain situations. Sometimes they think that if they don't know for sure they shouldn't even attempt to answer. They are afraid to put down a wrong answer.

   Tests are scored by the number of correct answers, so an educated guess is a no-lose decision. Take the time to explain how tests work and encourage your child to guess when it is helpful. If you have samples of test questions, you can demonstrate how to guess and why guessing works to the test taker's advantage.

   However, since the overriding goal is to learn and to find out what needs to be learned, point out that after the test your child should ask about what he or she didn't know.

6. Cope with mistakes and upsets.

   If a test is difficult or if a child feels that he is doing poorly, he may get so worked up that his emotions block his ability to think and answer. Children need skills to deal with negative self-talk and emotions so they can get back on track. They need to learn how not to "make a problem out of a problem" (see Chapter 11). Here is some self-talk that helps in these situations:

> "Don't panic! That won't help. It will only make it worse."
> "Concentrate! I can do it if I take my time and do it slowly."
> "This is only one test. One test doesn't make or break me. The only thing I can do is calm down and use my knowledge and skills the best I can."
> "If I don't do well I'll find out what I need to learn, study harder, pay more attention in class, or get help."
> "It's only one problem. Everyone makes mistakes."
> "Don't let it distract you. Concentrate on the answers you know."

Given enough time, these test-taking skills and strategies will work for your child. When Dr. Gordon Samson of Cleveland State University reviewed twenty-four studies on the effectiveness of training children in test-taking skills, he found that programs that continued for five weeks or more were very successful in alleviating test-taking anxiety.

These skills will help children to see tests as a challenge and a way to use what they've learned.

CHAPTER 10

POSITIVE PREPARATION THROUGH MENTAL REHEARSAL

> I NEVER HIT A SHOT, NOT EVEN IN PRACTICE, WITHOUT HAVING A VERY SHARP, IN-FOCUS PICTURE OF IT IN MY HEAD.
>
> JACK NICKLAUS
> *Golf professional*

> WHEN I POSE I'VE GOT A MENTAL PICTURE OF HOW I WANT TO LOOK. WHEN YOU HAVE THAT IN YOUR BRAIN THE PHYSICAL BODY JUST SEEMS TO RESPOND.
>
> RACHEL McLISH,
> *Women's World Body-Building Champion*

> I BELIEVE THAT FAILURE TO PREPARE IS PREPARING TO FAIL.
>
> JOHN WOODEN
> *Basketball Hall of Fame player and coach*

Proper preparation will propel a child into the achievement cycle. It gives the child the best chance of applying his or her talents and significantly reduces the pressure he or she feels about performing. In this chapter, I present relaxation, visualization, and mental rehearsal techniques that can be used to achieve these goals:

Obtaining a clear, detailed picture of the desired performance.

Anticipating obstacles and areas where further preparation is needed.

Increasing confidence through experiencing success mentally.

Reducing pressure and anxiety by making a mental "road map" and acquiring the "I've been there" feeling.

Achieving the benefits of practice and repetition.

LEARNING FROM THE PROS

Top performers take the time to prepare. Most of them overcome challenges and obstacles through systematic preparation. Your child can easily learn the preparation techniques used by professional athletes and performers and apply them in his or her academic, artistic or athletic pursuits.

Fran Tarkenton holds the National Football League records for total passes, completions, and yardage. Recently he revealed that before each game he imagined every play he was going to run. He pictured what the opposing players would do and how he would react. Fran repeated this process until he was confident that he had anticipated and prepared for each challenge he was going to face. Since retiring from football, Tarkenton has continued to apply these preparation techniques in various business ventures and has been spectacularly successful.

Likewise, tennis champion Chris Evert Lloyd reports that she anticipates all the significant details of upcoming matches and then mentally rehearses her desired play.

RESEARCH STUDIES

In addition to the testimonials of Tarkenton, Lloyd, and many other athletes and performers, we now have scientific evidence for the effect of mental rehearsal and preparation.

One study that created interest in mental practice used

teenage boys who wanted to improve their basketball foul shooting. One group actually practiced foul shooting. The other group sat in chairs and was encouraged to practice *mentally*. In their mind's eye they pictured themselves aiming, shooting, and even correcting for misses. When the two groups were tested, the researchers were amazed to find that the boys who "practiced" in their chairs improved almost as much as the boys who actually took foul shots.

This experiment demonstrated that significant learning can take place in our brains and muscles through mental imagery. Dr. Maxwell Maltz, author of *Psychocybernetics*, made a similar observation twenty-five years ago. He based his work on the idea that our brains react to vivid images with almost the same intensity as they would to real-life situations.

More recently, studies were conducted during the U.S. Olympic trials to determine the mental factors that contribute to achievement. Interviews with weight lifters revealed that the athletes who went on to qualify for the Olympics prepared mentally in ways that the nonqualifiers did not. The Olympic qualifiers devoted considerable preparation time to increasing *self-confidence, sharpening focus and concentration, creating the proper energy level,* and *visualizing the desired performance.*

However, visualizing—that is, producing mental images—can help us or hurt us. Researchers at Rutgers and Princeton Universities demonstrated both positive and negative effects of visualization in an experiment in golf putting. Two controlled groups of competing golfers were instructed to call up different mental pictures before each putt. One group imagined the ball going right into the cup; the other group pictured the ball going straight to the cup and then off to the side. The first group consistently outperformed the negative visualizers.

NEGATIVE MENTAL IMAGERY

Almost everyone practices some form of mental rehearsal. Before an exam, game or speech they picture *some* result, but it may not be positive. Instead of positive mental practice some of us conduct what psychologist Dr. Sandy Smith refers to as "dread rehearsal." "Dread rehearsal" is mental imagery, but all the images are negative. For example:

> "What if I miss these foul shots! We'll lose and everyone will blame me."
> "This is a dumb speech. I'm going to feel so stupid standing up there. I know they will see how nervous I am and start making fun of me."
> "She will probably give unbelievably tough problems. I'll never get them. I'm going to flunk. I hate math tests."
> "I'll never make it. I'm going to fail. I'll be so embarrassed."

Children and adults often don't realize that they are holding dread rehearsals; they are actually picturing themselves failing, over and over.

Worry and Fear

> *My life has been a series of terrible misfortunes . . . most of which never happened.* —Mark Twain

> *Cowards die a thousand deaths; the brave man dies but once.* —Shakespeare, *Julius Caesar*

People not only create vivid pictures of how not to do something; they also create worry and fear. When we feel fear, our bodies, minds, and nervous systems picture a painful event and then react almost as if it has happened. Fear is a form of mental imagery in which we picture negative things occurring and tell ourselves how horrible they would be.

Fear blocks even an adult's effectiveness, but we are better prepared to deal with it than children. For a child it often is the first stage of the underachievement cycle. Fear damages performance in these ways:

> *Negative focus:* Children can develop "tunnel vision" by concentrating on failure. It has a hypnotic effect, and soon they can't see any other outcomes to the upcoming event.
>
> *Wasting time and energy:* Worry robs children of valuable time and energy. While they are worrying they are not preparing or working on improving. Worry can exhaust them.
>
> *Demotivation:* For many children fear decreases the motivation to perform. If possible, they try to avoid the activity and usually decide that they don't like it.
>
> *Blocking skills:* Physical coordination and thinking skills are impaired when fear increases past modest levels. In this way fear becomes a self-fulfilling prophecy because now the child isn't able to hit the ball, solve the math problem, or speak in front of the class.
>
> *Negative self-message:* In addition to visualizing poor performance, a child pictures the negative reactions of his or her peers, teachers, or family members. He sees himself embarrassed or rejected. In this state he disregards his strengths, achievements, and resourcefulness.

Managing Fear with Positive Preparation

Worry and fear are signals that a child does not feel fully prepared. Problems result from getting stuck in fear. Our goal is to learn how to turn worry into anticipation, planning, and preparation. It is not necessary to eliminate fear completely. Moderate levels of tension, such as "butterflies," are a normal part of important events and can even be a useful source of energy and adrenalin. However, children can be helped to avoid or reduce the negative effects of fear through positive self-talk, relaxation, and mental imagery. And your child will be able to call upon these preparation skills of self-talk, relaxation, and mental rehearsal throughout his or her life.

Useful Self-Talk

Here are some examples of self-talk to help reduce the negative effects of worry.

> "Worry is a signal to me that I'm afraid of not doing well. I'm going to stop wasting time worrying and start planning and preparing for the challenges I face."
>
> "If I keep worrying like this I really will hurt my chances. My best bet is to concentrate on doing the best I can. I can always learn from my mistakes."
>
> "If I don't do well it won't be the end of the world. I'm exaggerating how awful it would be."
>
> "I've done things like this successfully before. I can do this, too."
>
> "I've had disappointments and setbacks before. If I have one this time I'll bounce back like I've always done."
>
> "The worst thing that can happen is I'll find out that I need to practice or study harder. No matter what happens I'll learn something and improve."
>
> "I'm ready. I'm prepared. I'm excited to get a chance to test myself."
>
> "I can pressure myself if I tell myself what a disaster it will be if I fail. I can take the pressure away by planning, preparing, and putting this in perspective. I control the pressure valve."

Greg Louganis, Olympic diving champion, practiced his version of self-talk during the final dive of the 1984 Olympic Games in Los Angeles. The pressure was at the highest point imaginable. Greg needed an almost perfect dive to win a gold medal for his team and give the United States the record for most medals won. He delivered: a perfect 10. Afterward he was asked about his thoughts as he scaled the tower. He said, "I was nervous but I said to myself, 'Greg, no matter what happens, your mother still loves you.' "

That is Greg Louganis's self-talk system for keeping performance in perspective.

RELAXATION TECHNIQUES

> *Mastery of some sort of relaxation technique may conceivably become a regular part of a child's educational experience.* —Georgia State Department of Education

Relaxation has two very important uses in mental preparation.

1. Often if a child is very nervous, trying to change his or her self-talk and focus will be only partially effective. Taking a few moments to relax and reduce tension levels will increase openness to positive self-talk.
2. It is difficult to practice positive mental rehearsal when you are totally immersed in "dread" rehearsal. Relaxing prepares the way for the clarity and control that make mental imagery so effective.

Relaxation is an important skill. Although children have many natural ways of relaxing (reading, listening to music, playing with pets, watching television, or kicking a ball), they can also benefit from learning specific relaxation techniques.

Touching and Massage

If a child is very upset about an upcoming test or event, it is often best simply to be close to and listen to her fears. If you both feel comfortable about it, gently touching her or softly massaging her muscles will help her calm down.

The love and support your child will feel through your hands combines with the loosening of tight muscles to create a very relaxed, receptive state. At this point the child will be more open to changing her self-talk and preparing in a positive way.

Deep, Slow Breathing

Controlling the rate of breathing is an excellent way to adjust tension levels. Breathing influences the pace of our thoughts. Deep, slow breathing calms the body and gives us an opportunity to take charge of our thinking.

A simple approach is to instruct a child to breathe deeply, all the way down to the stomach, and then let the air out slowly and evenly. After one of these long, slow exhalations the child is ready for another deep breath. The first few times a child practices this type of breathing, it may take three to five minutes before he starts to relax, but once he becomes skillful only a few breaths will be necessary.

Some children learn this technique better by making it into a "frozen rope" game. Ask your child to exhale slowly through his mouth and imagine that his breath is going out like a long frozen rope of air. This helps him concentrate and achieve a slow, even pace.

The Peaceful Place

If your child has a place where she feels peaceful and safe, you can ask her to take an imaginary trip there. This technique works best after she has lowered her tension through massage or slow breathing.

Each child's place will differ. It could be the beach, the woods, a park, a tree house, Grandma's house, or her own room. Going back to this place in the mind's eye recreates the relaxed, positive feelings she has there.

USING RELAXATION TECHNIQUES

Besides knowing particular ways of relaxing, it's helpful to know when they can be most effectively used.

The Night Before

If anticipating a test or game is creating so much tension that it interferes with preparation, suggest that your child take some time out to relax in his or her favorite way.

Just Before the Event

Watch professional athletes on television and notice how many stop and take a deep breath before they wind up to pitch, swing the bat, or take the foul shot.

Encourage your child to bring relaxation techniques right into the classroom and onto the playing field or stage. He or she can use relaxation to gain confidence and control before each exam or contest.

Before Mental Rehearsal

A relaxed mind is calm and open; it is primed for new, positive mental images. Relaxation aids the flow of images and helps the child direct his or her mental pictures in the desired direction.

MENTAL REHEARSAL TECHNIQUES

Dr. Charles Garfield, author of *Peak Performance*, has spent seventeen years researching the characteristics of peak performers. He believes that mental rehearsal is essential to each individual's reaching the performance level he or she is capable of achieving.

Children can adopt these techniques readily because they often imagine and visualize better than adults. Garfield stresses that these mental skills require practice because the best results come from achieving clarity and control over our mental images.

Warm-up Exercises

Although children use their imaginations regularly, they are unlikely to have any experience in directing and controlling their mental pictures. To introduce them to this activity, ask them to close their eyes and imagine a familiar scene (Grandma's house, a favorite bike route, the classroom). Invite them to examine this place in as much detail as possible. What are some of the sounds they hear there? How do they feel there?

Ask your child to think of certain animals or insects such as a turtle, a beaver, or an ant. First ask him to form a clear mental picture of each one. Then invite him to imagine the animal doing its work. What kind of worker is it? What is good about how it gets the job done? Encourage your child to visualize each animal completing a job. Take a minute or two for each.

The Main Event
After your child is comfortable with using her imagination, introduce her to exercises that will help her performance.

1. Visualize a previous success.

   Everyone can draw confidence from past achievements. As your child prepares for a new test or challenge, he may forget about other successes. This exercise helps to remind him that he has succeeded, and replays how he did it.

   The child should choose a successful experience that is as similar to the upcoming event as possible. If he has done well in this event before, this exercise will be especially helpful. Give your child these directions:

   > Mentally review your past success in step-by-step detail.
   > How did you feel?
   > What did you do?
   > Repeat the experience in your mind until you start to feel self-confidence.

2. Create positive pictures of the desired performance.

   Even before a child takes a test or tries out for the band,

she can picture herself performing the way she wants to. By seeing herself do well in detail she establishes a road map, a mental blueprint for success. The neuromuscular connections begin to form, and she increases the chance of attaining the results she wants. Going through each step in this way also gives her an "I've been there" feeling. It reduces the fear of the unknown. Give your child these directions:

> You are going to create positive pictures in your mind.
> First think about the task ahead of you.
> Think of all the different parts that are important to do it well.
> Now picture yourself step by step doing each part just the way you want to.
> See exactly how you will perform to get the results you want.
> Repeat this process several times until you have a clear image of your successful actions. Repeat this mental practice for five minutes at least twice a day, or more if you wish.

3. Search for obstacles.

Mental rehearsal is useful not only for practicing the right actions, but also to uncover obstacles or problems that haven't been prepared for. If a child gets stuck when trying to visualize his success, it is usually because he has uncovered an area where he is not confident. This discovery does not have to be discouraging. It is, in fact, a very useful discovery. Now the child knows where to spend more time and effort in preparation. He may need some tutoring or coaching.

4. Mentally practice overcoming obstacles.

Children are often afraid that a specific obstacle will arise. The fear of this one thing may undermine their confidence. They may ask:

"What if she asks that type of question?"

"What if he asks me to give my report out loud?"

"What if I forget the words I'm supposed to sing?"

"What if they're a lot bigger than us?"

"What if the whole tournament comes down to my match with their number one player?"

Through mental imagery a child can picture these problems occurring, but he or she can also visualize a strategy for dealing with them. You can help your child by:

Asking him or her if there are specific things he or she is afraid might happen.

Discussing different strategies or self-talk he could use to cope with each situation.

When he or she decides on the best reaction, inviting him or her to practice it.

You might use the following words:

"Visualize the event. Now picture the obstacle or problem occurring. See yourself coping with the problem. What are you saying to yourself? How are you feeling? What are you doing? Mentally practice how you will respond to the problem until you start to feel confident in your ability to deal with it. For example, how could you prepare for that type of question?"

"If you're required to give a verbal report, what could you do to make it easier?"

"If you forget some words when you sing, what's the best thing to do?"

"What strategy could you use to even things up if they are bigger than you?"

"If the tournament results depend on your match, what would be the most helpful self-talk to use?"

Most often the worst fears won't come true. Through mentally rehearsing coping strategies, your child will feel more confident and better prepared.

CHAPTER 11

SELF-MANAGEMENT SKILLS: NOT MAKING A PROBLEM OUT OF A PROBLEM

BE WILLING TO HAVE IT SO. ACCEPTANCE OF WHAT HAS HAPPENED IS THE FIRST STEP IN OVERCOMING THE CONSE-QUENCES OF ANY MISFORTUNE.

WILLIAM JAMES

During educational, athletic, and creative pursuits children run into different types of problems. Making errors, falling down, misspelling words, losing at games, not understanding the story, and getting stuck on math problems are regular, if not daily, occurrences. At times children simply don't do as well as they hoped.

Other problems are due to the unexpected actions of others. Children can be shaken easily by surprise quizzes, essay questions, poor calls by referees, or unexpected skill and strategy from an opponent.

These problems can be difficult, but they are usually manageable unless another type of problem is present, namely the child's emotional upset. When children (or adults) react to problems with high levels of fear, frustration, or discouragement, they have *two* problems. This process, which every human being experiences, is called "making a problem out of a problem." When we are upset, we add the upset to the existing problem and seriously reduce our chances of solving it.

If we are so nervous that our muscles are uncoordinated, if we are so frustrated that we don't think clearly about solutions, if we are so discouraged that we stop trying, we are well along the path to the underachievement cycle (see Figure 2, page 19). Thus, severe upsets can rob us of the very skills and resources we need to solve the problem at hand.

Thinking skills:	When we need to think creatively about possible solutions we have "tunnel vision" about poor performance and failure. ("This is so embarrassing. I'm awful at this.")
Physical skills:	When we need strength and coordination in our muscles and limbs, they feel frozen and awkward. ("I can't do it.")
Persistence:	When we need energy and endurance we feel tired and want to quit. ("What's the use? I'll never get it.")
Task-relevant thinking:	When we need our thoughts to be directed and relevant, we find ourselves thinking about things that really won't improve the situation. ("That's not fair. We never learned that." "That was a bad call. The referee is a jerk." "This always happens to us.")

We all make problems out of problems in this way. I teach and write about self-talk and self-management, and yet I make things more difficult for myself from time to time. While I am not guaranteeing perfection—total elimination of any unwanted upset—I can promise improvement.

While adults have acquired some skills in managing their emotions in difficult circumstances, children are generally unprepared. Children, as well as adults, can learn not to become upset as often, not to stay upset as long, and not to be as intensely upset if they feel that those upsets are blocking their ability to learn.

Remember that our goal is improvement, not perfection. Some keys to successful self-management include self-talk, concentration—including staying on track (task-relevant focus), solution consciousness, and persistence. We'll now turn to each of these.

THE SELF-TALK OF SELF-MANAGEMENT

The most important self-management principle children can learn is that they can alter their self-talk. They do not have to continue thinking and feeling as they do at a difficult moment. They can substitute more helpful thoughts by using the right self-talk.

This step is not easy, especially if a child is very upset, but with practice he or she can learn to reduce the upsets and feel the way he or she wants to feel more often. Some examples of useful self-talk include:

"I can change my self-talk."
"There are other, more helpful ways to deal with this problem."
"Being upset right now is making things worse. It's not helping me at all."

"I don't have to get rid of all my negative feelings. I just need to reduce them so I can start to move forward."

"What would be more useful for me to say to myself and do right now?"

"What would another child who wasn't upset do in this situation?"

"Don't take this too seriously.

CONCENTRATION

The first essential for the child's development is concentration. *It lays the whole basis for his character and social behavior.* —Maria Montessori, *The Montessori Method*

Maria Montessori obviously felt very strongly about the need for children to develop this ability, but how often are children actually taught how to concentrate?

Dr. Benjamin Spock reported recently that research into the lives of unusually successful people revealed a tendency, as children, to become deeply involved in activities. This finding raises questions. Were these people born with this tendency? Did their parents simply allow a natural process of absorption in activity to continue uninterrupted? Did these people receive some special training in concentration?

I don't know the answers to these questions, but I do know that children can be encouraged and taught to concentrate. It can be practiced at any time, and the child will improve with practice. It is a skill that will serve the child for his or her whole life.

Natural Concentration

Children naturally become absorbed in activity, and Maria Montessori built her educational model around this process. Montessori teachers encourage it, and the classroom is designed to allow it to occur.

Montessori's description of the child's ideal educational

state is remarkably similar to the childhood memories of Dr. Spock's successful subjects. She believed that a child seeks activities that involve his or her total interest. The child wants to be absorbed in "work accompanied by mental concentration." Once an activity draws his deep attention, the teacher or parent should allow him to pursue it.

Concentration Exercises

Certain activities are designed specifically to improve concentration. The "frozen rope" breathing exercise described in Chapter 10 can be used in this way; the goal is to focus the mind on an object for a period of time.

In *The Inner Game of Tennis*, Tim Gallwey suggests that players can benefit from simply staring at a tennis ball. Gallwey says that it heightens the power of concentration and helps a player "keep his eye on the ball" during the game. He adds, "Concentration is the supreme art, because no other art can be achieved without it, while with it, anything can be achieved."

I've used this technique in coaching first graders in soccer. Before we kick the ball around I ask them to stand in a circle. Then I put the ball in the middle and ask them to stare at it for one minute. They take it as a challenge and are usually able to do it. In this small way I prepare them to be alert and to watch the ball when they are on the field.

Staying on Track: Task-Relevant Focus

Professional athletes and performers have a variety of ways to contend effectively with pressure. One of the key skills in their repertoire is the power of concentration. Players in stadiums filled with 50,000 screaming fans often report that they didn't hear the crowd at crucial points in the game. Arnold Palmer once remarked that when he was putting, nothing existed for him except the ball and the hole.

In any situation we can focus on the task or we can have irrelevant, distracting thoughts. Children can learn from simple self-talk phrases that will help them stay focused on task. When performance problems develop, this self-talk will give them the best chance of using their full talents.

> "Let's take it one step at a time."
>
> "Now take a deep, slow breath. Let's shake off this feeling and get back on track."
>
> "Don't think about what might happen or jump to conclusions about how bad it is going to be. Concentrate on what you can do now."
>
> "I'm getting upset about something I can't control. I'm wasting my time and energy. I need to concentrate on things I can do something about."
>
> "These feelings are making things worse. I'll have plenty of time for bad feelings later. Now I've got to pay attention to what I'm doing and give it my best shot."

SOLUTION CONSCIOUSNESS

"Solution consciousness" is a set of mental attitudes common to achievers. Individuals who possess this quality spend more of their time and energy on "doing" than on "stewing." Although they may be disappointed or upset by setbacks, they don't get stuck. They "unstick" themselves by accepting the reality of the situation and then searching for ways to move forward. Thus those with solution consciousness do not simply accept the reality of a situation with mere helplessness. ("I can't do anything about it.") Rather they think, "It's happened. I can't do anything about the fact that it's happened, but I *can* concentrate on finding ways to improve it."

Solution consciousness is thus the "first step" that William James mentioned in the quote at the beginning of this chapter.

You can gradually teach your child the mental habits of moving from "stewing to doing," from upset to action. If a child gets stuck in negative emotions, he or she will stop gathering information about possible solutions. The key is to help the child shift focus to what can be learned or improved in each situation, or how he or she can prevent it from recurring. Examples of solution-consciousness self-talk include:

> "It's happened. I can't change that fact. All I can do is work out a plan to deal with it."
> "What can I learn from what has happened?"
> "How can I improve this situation?"
> "How can I prevent this from happening again?"
> "I can make something positive come out of this."
> "It's not going as well as I wanted. I need to get some feedback on how I can improve."

PERSISTENCE

Persistence is a key skill in overcoming obstacles of all sorts, whether they are emotional obstacles or performance obstacles. Persistence can be learned. Like a muscle, it gets stronger the more we put it to work. Children not only need to develop this quality; they need to realize that they possess the inner reserves that enable them to persevere.

In Chapter 8, I discussed ways of increasing self-discipline. These approaches also apply to developing persistence. Here are some additional self-talk phrases that can help children believe in their ability to stay with a challenging situation and improve it.

> "I have inner reserves."
> "I can do more than I think I can."
> "Stick with it. You'll feel great when you finish."
> "You're just starting out. You're new at this. Don't give up just because you aren't awesome yet. Keep at it."

"You've overcome obstacles before. You've learned hard things before. You can do it again."

"Problems help me learn. Overcoming adversity is going to help me reach my true potential."

SUGGESTIONS FOR TEACHING SELF-MANAGEMENT SKILLS

In this chapter I've discussed:

Not making a problem out of a problem
Self-management self-talk
Concentration
Task-relevant focus
Solution consciousness
Persistence

You can help your child acquire these skills and self-talk in the following ways.

1. Be a model of the desired behavior.

As mentioned earlier, direct observation is a compelling learning method. Take some time to read, study, and use the phrases and skills covered in this chapter so that you teach by example.

If you're driving with your child and get a flat tire, for example, you will probably be upset, but this is an excellent opportunity to teach solution consciousness. After you express your anger you might say, "Well, the tire is flat. No amount of cursing or being upset is going to change that. We need to figure out how to fix it or get help. I'd better check all the tires, too. Maybe they're getting worn and need to be replaced."

When your child sees you respond in this way, his or her mind will be prepared for learning how to deal with future "flat tires."

2. Discuss self-management strategies before problems arise. These are the essential ideas of self-management:

> Negative feelings, being distracted, and wanting to give up can block you from doing as well as you could.
> You can say things to yourself to feel differently, concentrate, and try harder.

Children ages six to ten can relate well to these ideas. They usually create their own version of the skills; more importantly, they learn that they can influence their feelings in a positive way.

Erika, a nine-year-old gymnast, had a fall while doing a vault during practice before an important meet. She was hurt and shaken, and thought of withdrawing. Her mother talked with her and explored her feelings, and it finally emerged that Erika wanted to compete but was afraid to vault. Erika competed in the three other events first and built her confidence. Then she faced her fear and vaulted. Surprisingly, her overall score was her highest ever. Afterward she proudly told her mom, "When I ran toward the vault I kept telling myself, 'Nothing bad happened, nothing bad happened.' " Erika found her own way to deal with that situation, and she also learned a mental skill that she will use repeatedly.

You can discuss self-management principles with your children before they face difficult circumstances. Use examples from television, movies, or books. When they are approaching a challenging task or test, help them think through a plan (including self-talk and actions) for handling any negative, blocking feelings they might have. You can think your child through an upcoming event by asking, "What could you say to yourself or what would be the best thing to do if this happened?"

Pam Lloyd, the riding instructor, prepares her students

for the uncertainties of competition by explaining that the horses are unpredictable and the judges' ratings are subjective. She tries to prepare them mentally in this way so that disappointments don't destroy performances.

3. Practice mental rehearsal.

To solidify self-management strategies you can call upon visualization and mental imagery techniques (see Chapter 10). A child can mentally rehearse coping with difficult events. He or she can picture problems arising and then see himself or herself using the self-talk and actions that create the greatest possibilities for improvement.

CHAPTER 12

LEARNING FROM EXPERIENCE: THE SELF-TALK OF IMPROVEMENT

EXPERIENCE CAN BE A GREAT TEACHER. BUT THERE IS A
BIG DIFFERENCE BETWEEN HAVING TEN YEARS OF EXPERI-
ENCE OR HAVING ONE YEAR OF EXPERIENCE TEN TIMES.
                                        WILLIAM BYRNE
                                    Real estate developer

Experience can be a good teacher, but not necessarily a teacher of good. Sometimes we don't learn anything and continue to repeat our mistakes. At other times we form the wrong conclusions about our abilities and potential.

DEALING WITH DISAPPOINTMENT OR FAILURE
Disappointment is an inevitable part of everyone's experience. If we know how to react to disappointments and setbacks, we're in a position to profit from our experiences. We can extract the most useful information from our setbacks if we learn the skills of obtaining accurate feedback and focusing our self-talk on improvement. The secret is to avoid the two extremes of self-downing and making excuses.

Self-downing   ⟷   Excuses
Self-blame   Blaming Externals

Self-Downing

"Self-downing" is a common practice after a poor performance: "Stupid," "Dummy," "You're a joke," "You'll never do it," "I'm awful," "I'm the worst one," "Why did you ever think you could do that in the first place?"

Self-downing always hurts and rarely helps. It is not self-improvement, it is not problem solving, and it often prevents both. This reality becomes even clearer when we see examples of self-downing in action later in this chapter.

Excuses

The other extreme reaction to disappointment is to make excuses. Not performing well can be painful to our egos. Finding ways to blame results on external factors is extremely tempting. Here are some typical excuses:

> "They were lucky."
> "She never taught us that."
> "The judge was blind."
> "Their coach cheated."
> "He doesn't like me so he gave me a bad grade."
> "It was too windy."
> "It wasn't my fault."
> "We lost because of her."
> "She was supposed to do it."
> "No one told me."
> "Those kinds of tests are stupid."

It would be hard to find someone who never makes excuses, and obviously there are times when excuses are valid. Still, problems develop when a person continually avoids personal responsibility for his or her performance. While an excuse may temporarily soothe the ego, it shows a lack of awareness about what the individual could do to improve.

Calm Self-Critique

The most useful way to react to disappointment or failure is with *calm self-critique,* a self-talk technique developed by Dr. Albert Ellis, coauthor of *A New Guide to Rational Living.* This technique helps a person examine his or her behavior and see what needs to be improved without excessive self-downing.

Calm self-critique:

Acknowledging disappointment
Putting event in perspective
Personal responsibility for results
Focus on learning
Focus on future
Seeking useful feedback
Realistic self-appraisal

Example: The Large Group Presentation

I can illustrate these three different reactions—self-downing, excuses, and calm self-critique—in an experience I had while I was working with Larry Wilson. Co-author of the best-selling book *The One-Minute Salesperson,* Larry is famous for his dynamic, hilarious motivational speeches.

In 1979 I developed some material and programs for Larry and for Wilson Learning Corporation, including a one-day event for a large West Coast bank. The bank expected 500 employees to attend. Larry always presented the material himself, but this time he said, "Marty, you designed a lot of this stuff. Why don't you get up there with me?" At that point in my career I had taught small seminars of 20 or fewer people, but hadn't made many presentations to large groups.

I accepted Larry's invitation, and we took turns presenting during the day. It was a long day. I bombed. I went "thud." A good friend of mine was in the audience, and he couldn't even muster up a smile. At lunch I overheard a woman saying, "Gee, I hope that guy Wilson gets back on in the afternoon."

My techniques, which worked well with 20 people, didn't work with 500. No one answered my questions. They weren't interested in my flip chart, and what the heck do you do with a microphone anyway?

Let's listen to the different self-talks I could have used in this situation.

Blaming myself. "What a disaster! This is the most embarrassing thing I've ever been through. I'm awful. Why did I ever think I could do something like this? What a jerk to get on stage with Larry Wilson!"

This is a great piece of self-downing. How would you feel if you said this to yourself? Did you hear me say anything so far that would help me improve? Actually all I did was decrease the chances that I'd ever attempt to speak to a large group again. Hence, self-downing can hurt you *and* your chance for improving.

Blaming others. "What a bunch of losers! I'm trying to give them some ideas that could help them and they aren't even interested. They'd rather have Larry come up and entertain them than really learn something. It's stupid even to try one of these programs where the president of the bank tells them to show up. They don't even want to be here. It's a waste of my time and energy."

That got me off the hook, didn't it? It's not hard to find excuses and blame other people. We've all heard some strange excuses and used a few ourselves, but what happens if blaming others for poor performance becomes a habit? I might feel better by using this self-talk, but the odds are very small that I would learn anything I needed to learn. When I blame other people, I'm not looking at myself either as part of the problem or as part of the solution.

Calm self-critique. "I'm really disappointed with how I did today. I misjudged so many things about working with a large audience, and the way I performed is unacceptable. I realize this is the first time I've done this, so I need to put my results in perspective. I know I have some strengths to build on. I'm articulate, I care about people, and I've got a good grasp of the material. Now I need to improve. I can see some things to do differently but I'd better ask Larry and some people from the bank to give me specific feedback."

This approach is really a skill, an extremely valuable, life-long skill that is the core of the attitude of a learner. Notice that in this self-talk I expressed disappointment but didn't destroy myself. I focused specifically on what I did wrong, but I put my performance in an overall perspective. By reminding myself of my strengths, I encouraged myself to begin to focus on improvement. I can't improve without the guidance of feedback. Individuals who practice calm self-critique achieve rapid progress. Their greatest edge is that most people avoid or reject feedback, while these people seek it actively and monitor their performance regularly.

In the actual situation I reacted in all three ways, but settled down to the attitude of a learner (after all, I was teaching this attitude). Larry and my friend in the audience focused my attention on ten things I should do differently. I listened, changed, and worked with Larry successfully many times after that. I'm grateful for the opportunity and for his honest feedback.

Let's see how these patterns apply to a child's world and

then learn how to help children acquire the self-talk of improvement.

EXAMPLE: THE ESSAY TEST

Charlie received a *D* on his first Social Studies essay test. Here are three possible reactions.

Self-downing: "Boy, am I a dummy. A *D!* My answers were stupid. They didn't make any sense at all. I just can't answer an essay question. I'm sunk from now on."

Excuses: "How could she give me a *D*? My answers were as good as Jill's and she got a *B*. This teacher always grades easy for the girls. Those questions were totally stupid. They didn't have anything to do with what's really important."

Calm self-critique: "A *D!* That's really disappointing. I know this was my first essay test so I don't want to be too hard on myself, but I definitely need to improve. I thought I knew the stuff we were tested on but I guess I didn't answer the way she wanted. I'm going to ask for help on how to answer essay questions and how to study for an essay test. From now on there will be more and more essay tests so I'd better figure out how to improve."

Note the key elements in the calm self-critique method:

> Acknowledging disappointment: "A *D!*" That's really disappointing."
>
> Putting the event in perspective: ". . . my first essay test . . ."
>
> Personal responsibility for results: ". . . need to improve . . . I didn't answer the way she wanted."
>
> Focus on learning: "I'd better figure out how to improve."
>
> Focus on the future: ". . . there will be more and more essay tests."
>
> Seeking useful feedback: "I'm going to ask for help . . ."
>
> Realistic self-appraisal: ". . . I don't want to be too hard on myself."

In the first chapter, when I described the experiences of Andrea and Jim, I gave you a preview of some of the skills you would learn. When Jim missed the shot and his team lost, he used a form of the calm self-critique. Let's review his self-talk to observe this approach.

> Acknowledging disappointment: "Boy, I wanted to make that shot . . . . It sure hurts to lose."
>
> Putting the event in perspective: "But I didn't lose the game. The team lost; it just came down to my shot."
>
> Personal responsibility for results: "I think I did rush the shot . . . . I didn't set up like I usually do."
>
> Focus on learning: "I'll just have to learn how to take my regular shot even with two seconds left."
>
> Focus on the future: "I'll get a lot more chances to hit important shots."
>
> Realistic self-appraisal: "All in all, I played a pretty good game. I know I tried as hard as I could."

In this example Jim didn't ask anyone else for feedback. He analyzed his own performance and felt that he knew what he had done wrong.

TEACHING THE CALM SELF-CRITIQUE APPROACH TO CHILDREN

1. Give feedback.

Incorporate the principles of calm self-critique when you give feedback to your child about his or her performance.

First, make every effort to talk to the child in private. Pete Rose has a vivid memory of his dad waiting *until they were alone* after a game and quietly asking Pete to evaluate his own efforts. After Pete finished, his dad added suggestions. Rose is firmly convinced that by offering criticism and advice in this way, his dad enabled him to develop his athletic potential and his overall attitude toward improvement.

Try to avoid the extremes of name calling or making excuses. Help your child to take at least partial responsibility for the results. Calm self-critique combines an attitude of responsibility with a focus on possibilities.

2. Point out examples of helpful and harmful self-talk.
If you're watching a tennis match with your child and a player calls himself names after missing a shot, ask, "Do you think that player is helping or hurting himself when he calls himself that name?" Most children immediately see that it feels bad and doesn't really help. You can follow up by asking, "What would help him to stop missing?" This question shifts the focus to improvement.

In a book, movie, or television show you may come across an example of someone who makes a lot of excuses and blames everyone or everything else for his or her poor results. Ask your child, "Do you think she will ever improve if she keeps making excuses? What would she have to do to get better?"

3. Be a model of calm self-critique.
Learn calm self-critique and use it in your daily life. After you've mastered the basics, apply them in situations where you didn't perform as well as you wanted to.

Start with tasks around the house and talk to yourself aloud so your child can observe. When your new cake recipe or carpentry project falls short of your expectations, talk yourself through calm self-critique. This will help your child to talk to himself or herself in the same way.

4. Encourage mental rehearsal.
Mastering the habit of calm self-critique is easier if you use mental imagery techniques. Instead of waiting until your next disappointing performance you can use all

your past disappointments for practice—or you can anticipate mistakes and rehearse how you will react to them.

> Select a situation where you performed or might perform poorly.
> Visualize yourself in the situation, not doing well.
> Picture yourself using calm self-critique self-talk.
> Repeat the self-talk until you feel accepting of yourself and have focused on receiving feedback and learning how to improve.

This technique is even more effective if you write out your calm self-critique message. Writing the message with your child provides an excellent opportunity to go over the key elements and principles. If a child is trying to learn calm self-critique for a particular sport or subject, encourage him or her to put the message on a 3 × 5 card and read it several times a day until it becomes a habit.

The Value of Feedback

In addition to critiquing yourself, getting feedback from others provides information and reinforcement that are essential to improvement. Practice is important, but you may practice your mistakes without even realizing it. Practice with accurate feedback leads to growth and development.

Feedback is so valuable that we ought to pay people for it, and yet many people avoid it. They are more interested in "protection" than "correction." You can set your child on the path to developing his or her full potential if you can create in him a receptiveness and openness to feedback. When he begins to seek it out, you'll know he is becoming a life-long learner.

Sources of Feedback

Feedback comes in many forms. Basketball hoops, tennis nets, test scores, mirrors, and booing or cheering all provide a type of feedback. These are some additional important sources of feedback:

> *Tapes:* Children can gain valuable self-awareness by watching themselves on videotape or listening to their singing or piano playing on cassette.
>
> *Charts:* Children can chart how often they do chores, homework, or exercise, or they can chart their improvement in foul shooting or reading books. Charts provide information and visual reinforcement of progress.
>
> *Asking for help:* It is very important to encourage children to seek information from peers, teachers, or yourself. Point out that most people like to help and share what they know.

SELF-EVALUATION QUESTIONS

Earlier I mentioned that Jim evaluated his own performance and determined what he needed to do to improve his clutch shooting. Self-detection and self-correction are highly desirable as a child becomes more and more responsible for monitoring his or her own actions. The goal is for a child to develop the attitude, "I know I can correct myself when I make mistakes."

Self-evaluation also includes learning from successes. Success reveals effective ways of doing things. By taking the time to analyze what we've done right, we reinforce that pattern as well as lifting our confidence.

Here are some simple questions your child can use for self-evaluation after an important game, test, or performance.

> "What did I do right? What did I do that I want to remember to continue doing?"

"What errors did I make? What should I do differently next
    time?"
"Was this a one-time mistake or is this a mistake I often
    make?"

As your child acquires these mental habits and skills, the
achievement cycle will predominate. Mistakes and setbacks
will be overshadowed by optimism and confidence in the
ability to improve.

A Final Word of Encouragement

As you complete this book you may feel overwhelmed, learning about hundreds of techniques, skills, and self-talk examples. You have read the results of years of research by many people so you shouldn't expect to apply it all immediately.

Encouraged by the knowledge that habits can be changed, skills can be developed, and attitudes can be improved, focus on the portions that seem most relevant to your family.

You have my best wishes for your family's progress on the path to performance without pressure.

References and Recommended Reading

Alschuler, Alfred S., Diane Tabor, and James McIntyre. *Teaching Achievement Motivation*. Middletown, CT: Education Ventures, 1971.

Benjamin, Carol L. *Writing for Kids*. 1st ed. New York: Harper & Row, 1985.

Bloom, Benjamin S., ed. *Developing Talent in Young People*. New York: Ballantine Books, 1985.

Briggs, Dorothy Corkville. *Your Child's Self-Esteem*. Garden City, NY: Doubleday, 1977.

Butler, Pamela E. *Talking to Yourself*. Briarcliff Manor, NY: Stein and Day, 1981.

Camp, B., G. Blom, F. Herbert, and W. Van Doorwick. *Think Aloud: A Program for Developing Self-Control in Young Aggressive Boys*. Unpublished manuscript, University of Colorado School of Medicine, 1976.

Connellan, Thomas K. *How to Grow People into Self-Starters*. Ann Arbor, MI: The Achievement Institute, 1980.

Coopersmith, Stanley. *The Antecedents of Self-Esteem*. Palo Alto, CA: Consulting Psychologists Press, 1981.

Dinkmeyer, Don, and Rudolf Dreikurs. *Encouraging Children to Learn: The Encouragement Process*. Englewood Cliffs, NJ: Prentice-Hall, 1963.

Dornbush, S. *Study of Stanford and the Schools, a survey of 7,836 students in six San Francisco Bay area high schools and 3,500 parents*.

Dreikurs, Rudolf, and Vicki Soltz. *Children: The Challenge*. 1st ed. New York: Duell, Sloan & Pearce, 1964.

Dubos, Rene J. *Celebrations of Life*. New York: McGraw-Hill, 1981.

Dweck, Carol S., and N. D. Repucci. "Learned helplessness and reinforcement responsibility in children." *Journal of Personality and Social Psychology.* 25:109–116.

Dyer, Wayne W. *What Do You Really Want for Your Children?* New York: Morrow, 1985.

Elkind, David. *The Hurried Child.* Reading MA: Addison-Wesley, 1981.

———. *All Grown Up and No Place to Go.* Reading, MA: Addison-Wesley, 1984.

Ellis, Albert, and Robert Harper. *A New Guide to Rational Living.* Hollywood, CA: Wilshire, 1977.

Emery, Stewart. *Actualizations You Don't Have to Rehearse to Be Yourself.* New York: Irvington, 1980.

Eyre, Linda, and Richard Eyre. *Teaching Children Responsibility.* New York: Ballantine Books, 1986.

Garfield, Charles, and Hal Z. Bennett. *Peak Performance.* Los Angeles, CA: Tarcher, 1984.

Goertzel, Victor, Mildred Goertzel, and Ted G. Goertzel. *Three Hundred Eminent Personalities: A Psychosocial Analysis of the Famous.* 1st ed. San Francisco: Jossey-Bass, 1978.

James, William. *The Philosophy of William James Selected from His Chief Works.* With an Introduction by Horace M. Kallen. New York: Modern Library, 1925.

———. *The Principles of Psychology.* New York: H. Holt and Company, 1893.

Harris, Amy Bjork, and Thomas A. Harris. *Staying OK.* New York: Harper & Row, 1985.

Johnson, Spencer, and Ann D. Johnson. *Value Tales.* La Jolla, CA: Value Communications, 1977.

Lickona, Thomas. *Raising Good Children.* New York: Bantam Books, 1983.

Loehr, James E. *Athletic Excellence: Mental Toughness Training for Sports.* Denver, CO: Forum, 1982.

Maltz, Maxwell. *Psycho-cybernetics.* New York: Pocket Books, 1969.

Maultsby, Maxie C., Jr. *Help Yourself to Happiness through*

Rational Self-Counseling. New York: Institute for Rational Living, 1975.

Meichenbaum, Donald. *Cognitive Behavior Modification*. New York: Plenum, 1977.

Meyers, Andrew W., and W. Edward Craighead, eds. *Cognitive Behavior Therapy with Children*. New York: Plenum, 1984.

Miller, Mary Susan, and Samm Sinclair Baker. *Straight Talk to Parents: How You Can Help Your Child Get the Best Out of School*. New York: Stein and Day, 1976.

Montessori, Maria. *The Absorbent Mind*. New York: Holt, Rinehart & Winston, 1967.

Moorman, Chuck, and Dee Dishon. *Our Classroom: We Can Learn Together*. Englewood Cliffs, NJ: Prentice-Hall, 1983.

Otto, Herbert A. *Guide to Developing Your Potential*. North Hollywood, CA: Wilshire, 1977.

Peck, M. Scott. *The Road Less Traveled: A New Psychology of Love, Traditional Values, and Spiritual Growth*. New York: Simon & Schuster, 1979.

Rosenberg, E. *Getting Closer: Discover and Understand Your Child's Secret Feelings About Growing Up*. New York: Berkley Books, 1985.

Rosenthal, Robert, and Lenore Jacobson. *Pygmalion in the Classroom: Teacher Expectations and Pupils' Intellectual Development*. New York: Holt, Rinehart & Winston, 1968.

Saunders, Antoinette, and Bonnie Remsberg. *The Stress-Proof Child*. New York: Holt, Rinehart & Winston, 1985.

Schmidt, Jerry A. *Do You Hear What You're Thinking?* Wheaton, IL: SP Publications, 1983.

Schuller, Robert H. *Tough Times Never Last, But Tough People Do*. Nashville, TN: Nelson, 1983.

Segal, Julius, and Zelda Segal. *Growing Up Smart and Happy*. New York: McGraw-Hill, 1985.

Seldman, Marty. *Self-Talk: The Winning Edge in Selling*. Granville, OH: Performancy Systems Press, 1986.

Spock, Benjamin. *Baby and Child Care*. New York: Pocket Books, 1957.

U.S. Department of Education. *What Works: Research about Teaching and Learning*. Pueblo, CO: Consumer Information Center.

White, Robert Winthrop. *Lives in Progress: A Study of the Natural Growth of Personality*. 3rd ed. New York: Holt, Rinehart & Winston, 1975.

Witmer, J. Melvin. *Pathways to Personal Growth: Developing a Sense of Worth and Competence: A Holistic Education Approach*. Muncie, IN: Accelerated Development, 1985.

Ziglar, Zig. *Raising Positive Kids in a Negative World*. Nashville: Nelson, 1985.

INDEX

Abbott, Jim, 92–93
Abilities. *See* Strengths
The Absorbent Mind, 44
Acceptance, 7–10
  of mistakes and imperfections,
    9–10
Achievement. *See also* Under-
    achievement
  case studies, 22–29
  cycle, 15–17, 20–22
  and learning, 40–41
  mental rehearsal for, 143–154
  persistence and, 15–16, 94,
    120, 161–162
  preparation for, 143–164
  self-esteem and, 7–8, 118–
    119, 120
  skills and attitudes of, 10–14
Actualizations, 41, 44
Affection, 9
Anorexia nervosa, 10
The Antecedents of Self-Esteem,
    118
Appreciation, 70–73
*Athletic Excellence: Mental
    Toughness Training for
    Sports*, 105

Attention, 9
Attitude, 31–32
  of learner, 41–43, 47
  toward mistakes, 43–44

Bandura, Albert, 20, 22, 86, 89,
    119
Baruch, Bernard, 51–52
Benjamin, Carol Lea, 91
Bennett, William J., 93
Blame, 168–169
Blom, G., 137
Bloom, Benjamin, 40, 109
Boiman, Donna, 95
Bolton, Robert, 85
Brainstorming, 63–64, 137–138
Branden, Nathaniel, 6
Breathing, deep, 150, 159
Briggs, Dorothy C., 8
Business, 40–41
Butler, Owen B., 40
Byrne, William, 165

Calm self-critique, 167–173
Camp, B., 137
Casals, Pablo, 80
Celebrations of Life, 43

182 • INDEX

Cheating, 127
Children, The Challenge, 44
Choice, 123–124
Chores, 128
Communication, 59, 73–79
Competency motivation, 7
Competition, 90
Concentration, 158–159
Confucius, 44
Connellan, Thomas, 118
Contributing to society, 120,
    127–128, 129–130
Control. *See* Self-control
Coolidge, Calvin, 94
Coopersmith, Stanley, 118
Coping, 119
Correction, 44–46. *See also*
    Feedback
Curiosity, 43

*Developing Talent in Young Peo-
    ple*, 76, 109
Disappointment, 165–171
Discipline. *See* Self-discipline
"Discounting," 64–66
Diversity, 99
Dornbush, Sanford, 96–97
"Dread rehearsal," 146
Dreikurs, Rudolph, 44
Dubos, Rene, 43
Dweck, Carol, 15, 16

Edison, Thomas, 42
Effort, 92–93
Ellis, Albert, 167
Emery, Stewart, 41, 44
Excuses, 166–170
Expectations, 73–79
External motivation, 103–109

Eyre, Linda and Richard, 81,
    128

Failure, 44–46, 165–171
Families, 59, 62
Fear
    of failure, 44, 45–46
    managing, 147–148
    mental imagery and, 146–147
Feedback, 44–45, 54, 96–99,
    171, 173–174
First-born children, 118–119
Ford, Henry, 15, 18
Forgiveness, 51–52
"Frozen rope" breathing exercise,
    150, 159
Frustration, 131–132

Gallwey, Tim, 159
Garfield, Charles, 41, 151
Getting Closer, 138
Ginott, Haim, 30
Goals, 46, 80–100
    setting, 81–85
    "stretch," 81–82
    winning, 103–104
Goertzel, Victor, Mildred, and
    Ted G., 41
Gordon, Arthur, 40

Habits, 31–32
Harris, Amy Bjork and Thomas,
    134
Help, 55
Herbert, F., 137
Hidden protectionism, 45–46
*How to Grow People Into Self-
    Starters*, 119
*How to Live Every Day of Your
    Life*, 51

The Inner Game of Tennis, 159
"Investing in Our Children: Business and the Public Schools," 40

Jacobson, Lenor, 73
James, William, 30, 155, 160
Johnson, Spencer, 50
Johnstone, Margaret, 51

Kienel, Paul, 52
Kroc, Ray, 120

Labeling, 60
Language, 48, 135
Learning. *See also* Skills
and achievement, 40–41
attitude of learner, 41–43, 47
characteristics of learner, 43–48
from experience, 165–175
methods, 48–52
observational, 52–57
self-talk, 47–48, 56
Levine, Melvin, 18
Lickona, Thomas, 56
Lloyd, Chris Evert, 144
Lloyd, Pamela, 95, 96, 163
Loehr, James, 105
Louganis, Greg, 148–149

Maine, Margo, 10
Maltz, Maxwell, 145
Massage, 149
Mays, Willie, 94
McAuliffe, Christa, 70
McLish, Rachel, 143
Meichenbaum, Donald, 135
Mental rehearsal, 143–154

and calm self-critique, 172–173
negative imagery, 146–149
techniques, 151–154
Meyer, Paul J., 101
Mistakes, 9–10, 43–44, 53
Montessori, Maria, 44, 158
Moore, John, 45
Mother Teresa, 34–35
Motivation. *See* Competency motivation; External motivation; Self-motivation; Success
Mozart, Wolfgang Amadeus, 109

Naber, John, 82
National Center for Exploration of Human Potential, 59, 61
Negative imagery, 146–149
Negative labels, 60
Nicklaus, Jack, 143

Obedzmski, John, 128
Oester, Ron, 75–76
Optimism, 43
Otto, Herbert, 59, 61, 62

Palmer, Arnold, 159
Peak Performance, 41
Peck, M. Scott, 116, 120
Peer Pressure, 121, 132–133
Penney, J. C., 46
Perls, Fritz, 85
Persistence, 15–16, 94, 120, 161–162
Pirsig, Robert, 34
Plimsoll point, 105
Problem solving, 46–47, 55–56, 134–139
Protection, 44–46

Raising Good Children, 56
Recognition, 70–73
Relaxation techniques, 149–151
    deep breathing, 150
    peaceful surroundings, 150
    touching and massage, 149–
        150
Remsberg, Bonnie, 118
Reppucci, N. Dickon, 15
Responsibility, 116–133
    assuming, 120
    and choice, 123–124
    guidelines for, 121–133
    nonoverlapping, 122–123
    and self-esteem, 118–121
Retton, Mary Lou, 34–35, 81
Risk taking, 45–46
The Road Less Travelled, 116
Roosevelt, Eleanor, 43
Rose, Pete, 75–76, 171
Rosenberg, Ellen, 132, 138
Rosenthal, Robert, 73, 74

Samson, Gordon, 142
Saunders, Antoinette, 118
Scanlon, Tara, 90
Schunk, Dale, 86, 89
Self-control, 119
Self-discipline, 116–133
"Self-downing," 165–166, 168,
        170
Self-efficacy, 22, 119
Self-esteem, 6–8, 10, 118–121
Self-evaluation, 126–127, 174–
        175
Self-management, 155–164
    concentration, 158–160
    self-talk of, 157–158
    teaching, 162–164

Self-motivation, 101–103
    attraction to activity, 102–103
    focus, 110–112
    self-talk, 110–115
Self-talk
    calm self-critique, 167–173
    case studies, 22–29
    focus, 34–37
    helpful and harmful, 172
    of learner, 47–48, 56
    listening to, 32–37
    and motivation, 110–115
    power of, 30–39
    to reduce worry, 148
    and self-management, 157–
        158
    teaching, 37–39
Shakespeare, William, 15, 146
Skills, goal setting and, 80–100
Smith, Sandy, 146
Social responsibility, 129–130
Solution consciousness, 160–161
Solutions. *See* Problem solving
Sophocles, 119
Spock, Benjamin, 107, 158, 159
Sports, 105. *See also* specific
        sports figures
Stone, Michael, 127
Strengths
    brainstorming about, 63–64
    communicating positive expec-
        tations, 73–79
    identifying, 58–79
    recognition and appreciation,
        70–73
    reducing "discounting," 64–66
    strength-acknowledgement
        method, 62–70
The Stress-Proof Child, 118

Success, 46
   creating, 85–96
   motivating power of, 86–87

Tarkenton, Fran, 144
Task-relevant focus, 159–160
Test taking, 139–142
Thoughts. *See* Self-talk
Touching, 149
Turner, Ted, 108
Twain, Mark, 58, 146

Underachievement, 15–17
   case studies, 22–29
   cycle, 18–20

Vaillant, George, 128
Value Tales, 50

Van Cott, George, 75
Van Doorwick, W., 137

Watson, Thomas J., 44
What Works, 93
White, Robert, 7
Wieland, Bob, 129
Wilson, Larry, 167–168
Witmer, Mel, 77
Wooden, John, 103–104, 143
Work, 128–129
Worry, 146–148
Writing for Kids, 91

Your Child's Self-Esteem, 8

*Zen and the Art of Motorcycle
   Maintenance*, 34